THE MIND OF THE MOURNER

The Mind of the Mourner

Individual and Community in Jewish Mourning

Joel B. Wolowelsky

OU**PRESS**

NEW YORK

Library of Congress Cataloging-in-Publication Data

Wolowelsky, Joel B.
The mind of the mourner : individual and community in Jewish
mourning / Joel B. Wolowelsky.
p.   cm.
ISBN 978-1-60280-149-3
1. Jewish mourning customs.   I. Title.
BM712.W66   2010
296.4'45—dc22
2010001251

Cover design: Pamela Walman
Cover art: Enya Keshet

Published by
OU PRESS
An imprint of the Orthodox Union
11 Broadway
New York, NY 10004
www.OUPress.org
OUPress@OU.org

Distributed by
KTAV Publishing House, Inc.
930 Newark Avenue
Jersey City, NJ 07306
Email: bernie@ktav.com
www.ktav.com
(201) 963-9524
Fax (201) 963-0102

This publication was made possible with the kind support of
the Goldstein Family

In loving memory of
Jamie Fischer

אביבה מאירה בת אלי' ע''ה

Her love of family and amazing support to all can never be replaced.
Her laugh and radiance will never be extinguished from our lives
and memories. She is missed every day since her passing.

Jamie's never-ending devotion and dedication to her son
Zachery was a testimony to Jewish Motherhood. Her
enduring legacy of love and life will continue to nurture
him in the months and years ahead.

May this volume help those who are mourning the loss of
their loved one as we are mourning the loss of our dear
daughter and sister.

Dedicated by her parents, Edward and Sheryle Goldstein
and her sister and brothers: Shelley, Todd, David and Jordan.

In memory of my parents

REBECCA AND IRVING WOLOWELSKY

לזכר נשמת

א"מ ישראל בן יואל בנדיט ומריידה ז"ל

א"מ רבקה בת זלמן וזיסל ז"ל

ת .נ.צ. ב. ה.

Contents

Publisher's Foreword

The OU Press is proud to be the publisher, together with Ktav Publishing House, of "*The Mind of the Mourner*," a volume which deals with the most fundamental aspect of the human condition, namely our mortality, in a way that highlights the sensitivity of classical Jewish tradition and the wisdom of our Sages.

Every mitzvah consists of two components, the *ma'aseh ha-mitzvah* (the external physical act of performing the mitzvah), and the *kiyum ha-mitzvah* (the actual fulfillment of the mitzvah). Rabbi Joseph B. Soloveitchik, the late preeminent rabbinic thinker of the twentieth century, noted that for many mitzvot, the performance of the *ma'aseh ha-mitzvah* itself accomplishes the *kiyum ha-mitzvah*, as the two components are merged into one integrated event. Examples of this type of mitzvah are taking the lulav on the holiday of Sukkot and eating matzah on Passover. In each case, the performance of the physical act—taking the lulav or eating the matzah—achieves fulfillment of the mitzvah.

Rabbi Soloveitchik further pointed out that there is another category of mitzvot, however, in which the *ma'aseh ha-mitzvah* and the *kiyum ha-mitzvah* are bifurcated. In these mitzvot, the *ma'aseh ha-mitzvah* consists of a physical act, but the *kiyum ha-mitzvah* consists of an internal experience, a *kiyum she-balev*, an emotional and psychological reaction that must take place in a person's inner being, without which the performance of the mitzvah is incomplete or completely void. Examples of this type of mitzvah are *tefillah* (prayer) and *teshuvah* (repentance). In the mitzvah of *tefillah*, the *ma'aseh ha-mitzvah* is the external act of articulating the words of the prayers, but the *kiyum ha-mitzvah* is the realization that one is standing before God. Similarly with the mitzvah of *teshuvah*, the *ma'aseh ha-mitzvah* is the recitation of *viduy*, the penitential confession, while the *kiyum ha-mitzvah* is the internal experience of regret, embarrassment and return to God.

A dramatic manifestation of a mitzvah in which the *ma'aseh ha-mitzvah* and the *kiyum ha-mitzvah* are separate and distinct is the mitzvah of *aveilut*. During the *shiva* period, the mourner is enjoined by specific prohibitions – no leather shoes, limitations on personal grooming, and so on. These prohibitions constitute the *ma'aseh ha-mitzvah*, but they do not extend to the *kiyum ha-mitzvah*. The fulfillment of the mitzvah of mourning must be found in the heart of the mourner; the sense of loss and grief is as important as the external physical acts. In truth, the psychological, emotional and cathartic experience is not ancillary to the institution of *aveilut*, but is the essence of *aveilut*, the means through which the pain and disorientation of bereavement are transformed into catharsis, consolation, and ultimately redemption. Without the emotional essence of the mourning experience, the external acts that comply with halakhic requirements are an empty shell devoid of meaning or substance. As the Mishnah in Tractate *Sanhedrin* states, *"Ein aninut elah be-lev*, the first stage of mourning, *aninut*, can be fulfilled only in the heart."

We are indebted to Dr. Joel B. Wolowelsky for *"The Mind of the Mourner,"* which delves into the psychological, emotional and philosophical aspects of the mourning experience. His penetrating insights give us all a deeper understanding of *aveilut* as well as a greater appreciation for the wisdom of our Sages in their approach to the ritual observances of *aveilut*. As he so persuasively and eloquently demonstrates, far from ignoring the emotional and the psychological, our Sages structured the halakhic framework of *aveilut* with the deliberate goal of addressing the emotional and psychological needs of the mourner. Feelings of overwhelming loss and tragedy, normal human reactions of guilt and resentment, the needs of the individual, the dynamic of the community – all of these are dealt with by the halakhic structure whose goal is understanding and sensitivity, as the volume clearly explicates.

An original and trenchant thinker, Dr. Wolowelsky has, over the years, made an invaluable contribution to the Jewish community through his role as a yeshiva educator, as one of the editors of *Tradition*, the Journal of Orthodox Jewish Thought published by the Rabbinical Council of America, as a prolific author on a host of issues confronting contemporary Jewish life, and as one of the editors of the Toras HoRav Foundation, which is dedicated to the publication of the works of Rabbi Joseph Soloveitchik. At his best in "*The Mind of the Mourner*," Dr. Wolowelsky takes the rabbinic literature dealing with death and mourning, distills its essence and demonstrates that the ritual structure expresses a consistent and coherent Jewish theology of death and mourning. The themes of this volume serve not only as a testament to our Sages' profound understanding of the human condition but also, to all who suffer bereavement and mourning, a source of comfort and solace. The OU Press is proud to include it in its library of significant works of lasting Jewish value. We also thank Mr. and Mrs. Edward Goldstein and family for their generous sponsorship of this book in memory of their daughter Jamie (Goldstein) Fischer, ע"ה.

Menachem Genack
General Editor, OU Press

Introduction

Mourning—the ritualized expression of grief—is a basic element of all societies, since a confrontation with death is a natural component of all human existence. Despite the universal aspects of this human experience, each society shapes the contours of its response in accordance with its own philosophical commitments and principles. Indeed, in many ways the mourning rituals express these societal standards as they concomitantly shape the community's response to death.

In the traditional Jewish community, mourning rituals are part of the general corpus of Halakhah, which is the system of law and religious practice that governs the everyday life of the committed individual. In this volume we explore these rituals and try to explicate their philosophical underpinnings.

The reader of these pages cannot help but notice the ubiquitous presence of the writings of Rabbi Joseph B. Soloveitchik, and this itself calls for an explanation and disclaimer. Rabbi Soloveitchik (1903–1993) was one of the preeminent Jewish thinkers of the second half of the twentieth century. So overarching was his intellectual presence that he was often referred to simply as "the Rav," that is, the Rabbi par excellence. He drew from a vast knowledge of Jewish and general traditions and championed the view that it was out of the sources of Halakhah that an understanding of Judaism and its principles was to be developed. The Jewish response to death and mourning was one of his recurring concerns,[1] and given his depth of psychological understanding and his eloquence of expression, it is hard to avoid drawing on his formulations in discussing the topic. Moreover, for more than a decade I have been involved in bringing the Rav's unpublished writings to print as part of the *MeOtzar HoRav* series of the Toras HoRav Foundation, and his words constantly echo in my ears.

Nonetheless, it would be unfair to consider this work as anything approaching a complete or systematic presentation of his views. Nor would it be fair to ascribe to him those thoughts and explanations in this volume that are not referenced to him. As large as my debt might be to his teachings and insights, the work remains a personal statement for which I alone must take responsibility.

In addition, it is important to note that this is not a practical compendium of contemporary Jewish law. Halakhah is a system of law, and as such it responds to the specifics of every individual situation. Mourners might find these pages

---

1. Many of his teachings on the subject have been collected in R. Joseph B. Soloveitchik. *Out of the Whirlwind: Essays on Mourning, Suffering, and the Human Experience*, ed. David Shatz, Joel B. Wolowelsky, and Reuven Ziegler (Toras HoRav Foundation, 2003).

valuable in understanding the overall ritual experience in which they are involved. However, the specific requirements of any situation demand the guidance of a rabbi or book of practical Halakhah.

Most of the ideas in this volume were first presented over the last four decades in my Jewish Philosophy seminars at the Yeshivah of Flatbush High School. I have been fortunate indeed to spend these many years with such a unique group of colleagues who are so dedicated, innovative, and knowledgeable; lay leaders who selflessly give of themselves in support of our mutual goal of excellence in Torah and secular education; and bright and inspiring students who make each day so pleasurable.

Over the years I have presented many of the ideas in this book in various journals, including *Bisdei Hemed, Death Studies, Hakira, Jewish Journal of Sociology, Journal of Family Social Work, Judaism, Le'ela, Morasha, Tradition,* and *Zohar.* I thank the editors of these publications for the opportunity they afforded me. The material has been reworked for this volume.

This book is being published by the OU PRESS and KTAV. I am grateful to Rabbi Menachem Genack, General Editor of the OU PRESS, and Mr. Bernie Scharfstein, Vice President of KTAV, for this opportunity and—more important—for their warm friendship. I am thankful to Enya Keshet for graciously sharing her creative artistic talent in helping to create the cover for this volume and for involving me in the preparations for her beautiful art book *Hadara: The Beauty of Women's Prayer.*

The Mind of the Mourner examines how the Jewish tradition helps people deal with their confrontation with death. May we soon see the day when "He will swallow up death for ever, and the Lord God will wipe off the tears from all faces" (Isa. 25:8).

Aninut

A Confrontation with Death

What thoughts and feelings pierce the hearts and minds of people confronted by the death of someone close to them? To be sure, the answers are as variable as the individuals involved, their time of life, and their specific relationships. Yet some themes seem to transcend individual circumstances. For example, often there may be a sense of aloneness, if not loneliness and even abandonment. There may be anger, directed at the deceased for leaving, at God for taking the person, at oneself for not meeting his or her responsibilities to the deceased, or "at life" in general. There may be concern for one's future that borders on selfishness. Living may seem to have no purpose, leading to withdrawal from life's adventures as people confront their own mortality. As John Donne said, "Any man's death diminishes me, because I am involved in mankind; and therefore never send to know for whom the bell tolls; it tolls for thee."[2]

---

2. John Donne, "Devotions upon Emergent Occasions" (1623), XVII.

The tradition does not merely note these emotions and reactions; it is committed to an honest confrontation with them. Stoic justification of God's judgment without emotive response is simply inappropriate. It is instructive to note the response of Rabbi David ben Solomon ibn Zimra "regarding one of the leading authorities of the generation who lost a son but did not shed a single tear over him."

> This is an evil trait demonstrating hardness of the heart and wickedness of the soul. This is the trait of cruelty, the way of philosophers who claim that this world is merely an illusion. They are diminished by their vanity . . . One who cries and mourns and sheds tears over the deaths of relatives—and all the more so over a fitting person—[reflects] the trait of the pious, the prophets, and men of deeds.[3]

Death triggers *aninut* (the mourning period that extends from the initial confrontation with death until the burial of the deceased) and with it a series of specific halakhot, the most dramatic of which is the exemption from all positive mitzvah obligations, including the requirement of daily prayer. At first glance, this exemption simply flows from the principle that one who is engaged in performing one mitzvah is exempt from the obligation to perform another. Since the *onen* (the term for the mourner during the period of *aninut)* is obligated to arrange for the burial of the deceased, the Halakhah exempts him or her from other obligations. But for Rabbi Joseph B. Soloveitchik, this exemption is to

---

3. R. David ben Solomon ibn Zimra, *Responsa Radbaz* III:555.

be understood in light of the psychological dynamics of the mourner's initial unmitigated confrontation with death.

> *Aninut* represents the spontaneous human reaction to death. It is an outcry, a shout, or a howl of grisly horror and disgust. Man responds to his defeat at the hands of death with total resignation and with an all-consuming masochistic, self-devastating black despair. . . . Are we not, the mourner continues to question himself, just a band of conceited and inflated daydreamers who somehow manage to convince themselves of some imaginary superiority over the brutes in the jungle?[4]

This feeling, he suggests, is the rationale for exempting the *onen* from all the positive commandments. "In a word," he summarizes, "the motto of *aninut* is to be found in the old pessimistic verse in the book of Ecclesiastes (3:19): 'So that man has no preeminence over the beast, for all is vanity.'"[5] The sickening feeling that one's life has no greater meaning than that of the anonymous animal is expressed in the exemption from positive mitzvot. Demands cannot be made on people unless they feel that their actions count. What point is there in requiring an *onen* to recite a blessing if he or she cannot imagine that there is significance to anything? Going on as if nothing had happened is dishonest; yet, on the other hand, lashing out is not healthy. The *onen*

---

4. R. Joseph B. Soloveitchik, "*Aninut* and *Avelut*," in *Out of the Whirlwind*, pp. 1ff.

5. Ibid.

remains obligated to refrain from any positive action that would violate Jewish law.

No Preeminence over the Beast

The Halakhah does not simply recognize these feelings of despair; it demands that they be acknowledged. It is almost as if the tradition insists that it would dishonor the dead to declare that a confrontation with death does not shake one's faith. The *onen* is exempt from praying, and if he or she insists on praying, "Amen" is not recited in response to blessings said. Indeed, the *onen* cannot be counted in a *minyan,* the quorum of ten required for public prayer. So too is the *onen* excluded from participating in the quorum required to recite the *zimmun* introduction to *Birkat ha-Mazzon,* the "Grace after Meals."

> Man has the choice to eat either in hiding, alone, like the beast in its lair, or in community, before the Lord. . . . The idea which this *halakhah* tried to translate into a ceremonial is that of a community formed by the act of eating. The *se'udah* [formal meal] is designed not only to satisfy man's physical needs, but also to take him out of his sheltered seclusion and loneliness and let him join the thou. Eating becomes a cohesive force bringing together people who were shut up in their own small worlds and coalescing them into a community.[6]

6. R. Joseph B. Soloveitchik, "An Exalted Evening: The Seder Night," in *Festival of Freedom: Essays on Pesah and the Haggadah,* ed.

The *onen*, unable to see him- or herself as part of that human community, is excluded from the quorum enabling the *zimmun's* recitation

We note that the less-than-human status of the *onen* is further reflected in the prohibition against eating meat. If this prohibition stemmed from the fact that eating meat is a sign of joy, there would be no reason for it not to extend throughout mourning rather than have it end with burial of the deceased. Rather, we suggest, the proscription is a substitute for the prohibition against the *onen's* wearing leather shoes, something that reflects human status. Generally, all the restrictions of the later *shiva* period are in effect during *aninut* as well. But the *onen* is required to go about in order to arrange the deceased's funeral and burial and must be able to wear sturdy shoes.

The daily series of morning blessings which we now recite as a unit were originally said individually in response to specific stimuli. The blessing *"she-asa li kol tzarki,* who has provided for my every need" was recited upon putting on one's shoes. There is a hierarchy to nature, explains Rabbi Isaiah ben Avraham Ha-Levi Horowitz, and humans are at the top. Animals eat vegetables; humans eat and exploit animals.

> When man takes the skin of an animal to make soles for his shoes, he demonstrates most dramatically that he rules over all and that everything is under him. This provides for

Joel B. Wolowelsky and Reuven Ziegler (Toras HoRav Foundation, 2006), p. 21.

all his needs, as he rules over everything. Thus when he puts on his shoes he says the blessing "who has provided for my every need."[7]

Indeed, the Talmud[8] records the aphorism that a Sadducee addressed to R. Joshua ben Karhah: He who has shoes on his feet is a human being; but he who does not is as good as dead.

On Shabbat, as we shall later discuss, all mourning is to be done privately. Hence the mourner would be allowed to wear leather shoes on Shabbat and, indeed, the *onen* may eat meat on Shabbat. The prohibition against eating meat expires with the burial of the deceased, when the *onen* no longer has an exemption from the prohibition of wearing leather shoes.

Tosafot[9] tie the *onen*'s prohibition to eat meat and drink wine to the obligation to not be distracted from the task of burying the dead. Yet wine can be more than a distraction; it can be a numbing agent. Emmanuel Levinas's comments

---

7. R. Isaiah ben Avraham Ha-Levi Horowitz (known as the Shelah, after the title of one of his major works, *Shnei Luhot Ha-Brit*), *Siddur ha-Sh'lah*, s.v. *"She-asa li kol tsarki."* Note also the Talmud's suggestion (Pesahim 49b) that a brute and boorish *am ha-aretz* may not eat meat. It is one's status as a full human being that allows a person to eat meat, and one who forfeits that status thereby forfeits the permission to eat meat. See R. Yehuda Levi ben Bezallel (Maharal mi-Prague), *Netivot Olam, Netiv HaTorah* 16, and R. Meir Simha Ha-Kohen mi-Dvinsk, *Meshekh Hokhma, Beha'alotkha* (Numbers 11:18).

8. Shabbat 152a.

9. Moed Katan 23b, s.v. *ve-eino okhel bassar.*

on why the *nazir* (the nazirite who took the ascetic vow described in Numbers 6:1–21) may not drink wine apply well here.

> Why the prohibition against wine? Because drunkenness is an illusion, the disappearance of the problem, the end of responsibility, an artificial enthusiasm; and the nazirite does not wish to be deceived, or to be relieved of the weight of existence by forgetting Evil and misfortune. Lucidity, realism, absolute fidelity in a lucid state and not drunkenness and exaltation.[10]

A confrontation with death demands courage and realism, not an artificial retreat from the problem.

An Angry Tear

Mourners may normally experience anger as a reaction to death, and, indeed, this anger is not necessarily completely rational. There may be anger toward the deceased for abandoning and "inconveniencing" the survivors, and even anger toward themselves—guilt—either for feeling that anger or for not having done enough for the deceased. Similarly, there may be anger toward God for allowing this to happen, and—especially for a religious person—this reaction too might create feelings of guilt. The language of *Shul-*

---

10. Emmanuel Levinas, *Nine Talmudic Readings*, trans. Annette Aronowicz (Bloomington: Indiana University Press: 1990), p. 123.

han Arukh suggests that *keriyah* is a *response* to justifying God's actions with the recital of the blessing proclaiming Him to be *Dayan Emet*, a true judge, almost as if being forced to describe the event as God's justice necessitates the cathartic release of *keriyah*. "*Tziduk ha-din* [justifying God's actions] is said at the time of death, and when he gets to [the end of the *berakhah*] '*Dayan Emet*' the mourner tears [his garment]."[11]

On the surface, *keriyah* might simply symbolize the torn heart of the mourner. "Mourning symbolizes a torn emotional unity, love which has no outlet, despair at the incompleteness of one's existence, at something which was torn out of one's very existence."[12] However, a Talmudic discussion[13] regarding the laws of Shabbat gives us added insight into the dynamics of this practice.

The Mishnah relates tearing one's clothes on Shabbat in a fit of anger to doing *keriyah* on Shabbat as an act of mourning. While one would normally not be fully culpable as a Sabbath desecrator for a prohibited act that is of a destructive nature, Maimonides[14] rules that such tearing of one's clothes in a fit of anger on Shabbat is a *constructive* act inasmuch as it is a cathartic action which settles the

---

11. R. Yosef Karo, *Shulhan Arukh, Yoreh De'ah 339:3*.

12. R. Joseph B. Soloveitchik, "Marriage," in *Family Redeemed*, ed. David Shatz and Joel B. Wolowelsky (Toras HoRav Foundation, 2000), p. 55.

13. Shabbat 105b.

14. Maimonides (Rambam), *Mishneh Torah, Hilkhot Shabbat,* 10: 10.

agitated mind. His ruling is based on this Gemara's discussion, where a second principle is established: venting anger is constructive if the expression is controlled; uncontrolled rage is akin to idolatry.

We have, then, a key to an understanding of the function of *keriyah*. This ritual tearing of one's clothes is hardly a spontaneous release. For example, the tear must be done while standing, be of a particular length, and be at a particular place on one's clothes. *Keriyah* allows emotions that may border on frightening rage to be expressed as controlled, healthy anger. It both permits the bereaved to express these feelings and teaches that it is neither uncommon nor uniquely wicked to have them.

There is another dimension to *keriyah*, one that reflects the feeling that man has no preeminence over the beast. Human dignity is expressed by wearing clothes. People clothe themselves; the brute does not. Indeed, the priest's garments actually affect his personal status: It is whenever they don their priestly garments that *kehunatam aleihem*, that they have their status as *kohanim* (priests).[15] *Keriyah* simply rips the clothes, but it symbolically rips them off. The confrontation with death deprives humans of their dignity, and they forfeit the dignity of unripped clothes.

Despite the fact that *keriyah* is mandatory, it is not preceded with the traditional blessing "who has sanctified us with His mitzvot and commanded us to. . . ." This omission is not to be explained by the general exemption of the

---

15. Sanhedrin 83b, Zevahim 17b.

onen from saying blessings; rather it is required by the general logic of introducing a mitzva*h*-act with a blessing. The rabbinic position[16] is that mitzvot done out of a sense of halakhic obligation have greater religious import than those done in a response to an inner personal calling. For example, one might enjoy eating by candlelight because of the mood it creates. But as the Sabbath approaches, one recites the *berakhah* to emphasize that the later evening meal will be eaten by candlelight because it is an obligation to do so, even if one's personal preference would be otherwise.

This principle, however, was not necessarily extended to every mitzvah. For example, in explaining why no *berakhah* precedes the sending of *mishl'ah mannot* ("presents" of food) on Purim, Rabbi Yehiel Yaakov Weinberg[17] argues that since the purpose of this mitzvah is to create and strengthen friendships, to precede it with the phrase "who commanded" and thereby indicate that the gift was the result of religious obligation rather than personal feelings would—contrary to the general principle—cheapen the moment.

Thus there is no *berakhah* for *keriyah*, despite its obligatory nature. A *berakhah* would detract from the respect due the deceased to suggest that the sweep of emotions expressed through *keriyah* is mandated rather than freely felt. Indeed, the association of this obligation with *kibbud ha-met* (the honor automatically due a dead person by virtue

---

16. Kiddushin 31a.
17. R. Yaakov Weinberg, *Responsa Seridei Eish* 2:46.

of his human status) explains the fact that while an *onen* is exempt from all positive obligations, the mourner is (generally) required to do *keriyah* before the *onen* period has ended. The *onen's* original exemption is part of *kibbud ha-met*;[18] one would therefore not be exempt from *keriyah*, which itself is part of *kibbud ha-met*.

Interestingly, one must do *keriyah* if present at the actual death of *any* individual.[19] It is not that the passing of this anonymous person evokes a sense of anger or sorrow. *Keriyah* here is mandated behavior, not directed emotion. It is an acknowledgment of our values—in this case our commitment to the infinite value of human life. One may have a dispassionate awareness of the inevitability of death, but one cannot witness an actual death without acting out a sense of loss—and a preparatory *berakhah* would likewise be inappropriate for such an action.

Yet in this case the Halakhah has tempered its theoretical concerns with a sense of reality. Sadly, in our contemporary society insisting on this requirement of *keriyah* might actually drive people away from staying with a dying person: the thought of having to ruin one's jacket might blind human sensitivities and dissuade one from staying.[20] The Halakhah cannot tolerate a requirement that might condemn a person to a lonely death.

---

18. J.T. Berakhot 3:1.

19. *Shulhan Arukh, Yoreh De'ah* 340:5.

20. R. Yekutiel Yehudah Greewald, *Kol Bo al Avelut* (New York: Feldheim, 1965), p. 26, paragraph 2.

Two Berakhot

There are two blessings whose recitation is required upon hearing of the death of one's parents.[21] The first obligation is well known, the second more obscure.

The "popular" *berakhah*, so to speak, is the *Dayan Emet* blessing which proclaims God to be the "True Judge." One of the purposes of blessings is to refocus our view of the world. In a sense, they are designed to express what we do *not* feel. When people go to the lavatory, for example, they are for the most part oblivious to the majesty of a well-functioning human body; hence the requirement for a *berakhah* that calls our attention to the fact that we are indeed fragile. When we hear thunder, we think to rush inside to a man-made protective shelter; hence a *berakhah* recognizing that "God's grandeur fills the world." When death strikes, we immediately focus on the apparent injustice; hence a *berakhah* recognizing God's justice. Indeed, the *Dayan Emet* blessing, by creating an intellectual dissonance between our gut reaction and our intellectual commitments, forces us to come to grips with our conflicting reactions.

The second *berakhah*, the one whose obligatory recitation is generally not well known, is *Sheheheyanu* (or *Hatov ve-Hameitiv*), the *berakhah* that is recited upon hearing good news or feeling great personal joy. What triggers the *berakhah* here is not the news of death, but the realization that one has inherited one's parent's estate. Whether riches come

---

21. Berakhot 59b; *Shulhan Arukh, Orah Hayyim* 223:2.

from winning the lottery or benefiting from a life insurance policy, one is required to thank God. At first glance, we may admit, this seems a bit offensive. Surely this is not the time to focus on one's selfish reaction!

When the great ethicist of the Slabodka Yeshivah, the "*Saba (Alter) MiSlabodka,*" Rabbi Natan Zvi Frankel, was asked about this matter, he responded by focusing on the importance of acknowledging selfish reactions. He took note of the Ashkenazic custom *not* to recite *Sheheheyanu* at the *brit* (circumcision) of one's son, commenting:

> To what extent did *Hazal* penetrate the innermost depths of the person! Here he makes a celebration, singing joys to God and man. But they said to him: Don't say the *Sheheheyanu* blessing, because deep inside you are pained [that your son will suffer during the *brit*]. And here he cries, rips his clothes and mourns; yet they said to him: Say the *Sheheheyanu* blessing, because deep inside you are pleased that you received this inheritance.[22]

Indeed, the issue is not the inheritance, but the many selfish reactions death triggers. We worry about how we will survive financially; we sometimes are relieved of the burden of caring for a sick relative, and so on. These are not necessarily the noblest of emotions, and we might be afraid to admit them to ourselves, let alone to others. But the requirement to say this blessing expresses the necessity of bringing those internal responses to the surface so they may

---

22. Quoted in *Hayei ha-Musar,* ed. the students of Yeshivat Beit Yosef (Bnei Brak: Hokhmah u-Musar, 5723 [1963]), p. 70.).

be confronted. When one has a secret too terrible to tell, it owns him or her. When the secret can be put out in the open, we learn to deal with it. If we don't like the way we are reacting, we can begin to work on ourselves. Requiring the recitation of *Sheheheyanu* does not endorse these feelings of selfishness but forces them to be acknowledged.

In general, the *onen* may not recite *berakhot*. We understand that *Dayan Emet* must be recited nonetheless, because its recitation is part of the mourning obligation—just as the mitzvah of *keriyah* remains in effect despite the mourner's exemption from performing positive mitzvot. Reciting *Sheheheyanu* (or *Hatov ve-Hameitiv)* is likewise not exempted, because recognizing and expressing these conflicting feelings are part of the obligations of the mourning process. Realizing that these are universal feelings—that everyone says this blessing—makes them easier to admit and confront.

As a practical technical matter, this *berakhah* is not usually recited nowadays, apparently because the current probate laws have created a reality where notice of death does not bring with it immediate inheritance. But this does not deny the basic truth that the original halakhah reflects.

The Hevra Kadisha

While the laws of *aninut* give expression to the *onen's* feeling that "man has no preeminence over the beast, for all is vanity," the community quickly acts to maintain the status of humans as created in the image of God. The *Hevra Kadi-*

sha, the "Holy Brotherhood" made up of men and women whose charge it is to care for the body now devoid of its holy soul, acts to protect the human dignity of the corpse, which retains its own holiness. The halakhic view that the body retains its sanctity after death is illustrated by the halakhah that something that housed or adorned a *sefer Torah* retains holiness when the Torah is removed and may not be used for a "lower" purpose.[23] The *sefer Torah* adornments, however, may be used as shrouds for an abandoned corpse, a *met mitzvah* that must be buried by the community; after all, the body, now devoid of life, had housed a human soul.

The corpse becomes a commanding presence in the hands of the *Hevra Kadisha.* A *shomer*—a religious honor guard, so to speak—is appointed to stay with the body until it is buried. The *shomer* guards the dignity of the cadaver, not its physical shell, guaranteeing its status as a non-abandoned *human* body. One may not speak in the presence of the body, except for matters that pertain to its needs. One may not even pray in its presence, for to do so is to mock the fact that the desceased can no longer pray. (The *shomer* simply sits by the body saying *Tehilim,* relying on the Psalmist to find appropriate words at a time when no words would suffice.) This restraint extends to preparing the body for burial: one does not hand something over the corpse lest it be interpreted as indifference or disrespect.

The body is carefully washed and then ritually cleaned by pouring water over it or immersing it in a *mikveh.* This

---

23. *Shulhan Arukh, Orah Hayyim* 154:3–6.

ritual cleansing of the corpse—*taharat hamet*—has a paradoxical inversion nature to it. In general, water is used to purify a person who has come in contact with a corpse (Num. 19:14–19), but here the object of purification is the corpse itself, the *avi avot ha-tumah*, the primary source of ritual defilement. The *Hevra* members call out "*Tahor hu/ tahora hi*, He/ she is pure." Of course, the corpse cannot be cleansed of its *tumah*, but we treat it as if it could, because we will not quickly forfeit its human status.

The deceased is then dressed in simple hand-sewn shrouds loosely patterned after the garments worn by the High Priest during the Yom Kippur Temple service. They consist of a head covering called a *mitznefet* (the same term used in the Bible for the priest's miter), a shirt, trousers, coat, and belt. A woman's face is covered with a veil and a man's with a *tallit* (prayer shawl).

As they work on enrobing the body, the *Hevra* members intone various biblical verses, again suggesting the paradoxical inversion motif:

> I will greatly rejoice in the Lord, my soul shall be joyful in my God; for he has clothed me with the garments of salvation, he has covered me with the robe of righteousness, as a bridegroom decks himself with a garland, and as a bride adorns herself with her jewels. (Isaiah 61:10)

> And I said, Let them set a pure miter on his head. And they set a pure miter on his head and dressed him with garments. And the angel of the Lord stood by. (Zechariah 3:5)

> And with the linen miter shall he be attired (Leviticus 16:4).

Far from being a discarded shell, the corpse is considered royalty, as are the bride and groom under their *huppah*. Like the High Priest, he or she will soon stand before the Holy One, purified.

The *Hevra Kadisha* protects not only the dignity of the deceased; it also protects the self-esteem of the living. It is so ingrained a custom that it seems natural for us to use unadorned clothes and a simple coffin. Death is the great leveler, and it is our good name and not our jewelry that we take with us when we leave this world. However, it was a consideration of *hesed* that motivated the Rabbis, not some abstract philosophical principle.

> Formerly, they used to uncover the face of the rich and cover the face of the poor because their faces turned livid in years of drought. The poor felt shamed, and they therefore instituted that everybody's face be covered, out of deference to the poor. . . .
>
> Formerly, they used to bring out the rich for burial on a *dargesh*, a tall bed ornamented with rich covers, and the poor on a plain bier. The poor felt shamed, and they therefore instituted that all should be brought out on a plain box, out of deference to the poor.[24]

We often hear people railing against false values, but it takes a real leader to step forward to use his or her own personal collateral to serve the best interests of the community. To set an example, Rabban Gamliel, the wealthy head of the

---

24. Moed Katan 27a–27b.

Jewish community whose social status surely called for a lavish final honor, prescribed the manner of his own funeral

> Formerly, the expense of burying the dead was harder for a family to bear than the death itself, so that the relatives abandoned him and fled, until at last Rabban Gamliel came and, disregarding his own dignity, was taken out in simple linen vestments, and thereafter the people followed his example to be buried in simple linen vestments.[25]

So significant was Rabban Gamliel's action that the Rabbis instituted drinking a cup of wine at the mourner's home in recognition of his action.[26]

In a final gesture to the still-human status of the dead before them, the members of the *Hevra* address the deceased by name and continue:

> We ask for forgiveness from you if we have not handled you with the respect owed you, but we have acted in accord with the custom of this place. Go in peace, and be an advocate for us and all the People of Israel.

In Israel, the body is taken on a plain bier to the cemetery. Elsewhere, the deceased is placed in a simple wooden casket into which soil from the Land of Israel has been placed, and the body is brought to burial.

There is an obligation to bury the dead as quickly as possible, yet there is a deliberate choreography that slows

---

25. Ibid. 27b.
26. Ketubot 8b.

the process. No one filling in the grave hands the shovel to another. Instead, each puts the shovel down and another picks it up. There is no work crew here rushing to fill a hole. Rather, each person comes humbly to do personally what he or she can, and then simply falls back when he or she can do no more. In many places, the back of the shovel's blade is used initially; burying a human being requires a hesitant gesture. Once the body or casket is covered, shoveling is then continued quickly. The mourners too have a right—to get on with their life as quickly as possible. Then, with another nod to the dignity of the deceased, a mound is placed atop the grave, signifying its human contents.

With burial, the period of *aninut* comes to an end.

Avelut

Master of Deed and Emotion

If the period of *aninut* expresses the determination of the Halakhah to compel expression of the various emotions and feelings—be they anger, selfishness, despair, or worthlessness—that seem to contradict our basic religious and existential assumptions, then the period of *avelut*, which begins with the burial, reflects the Halakhah's resolve that the mourner not be trapped by these feelings. "With the commencement of *avelut*," says Rabbi Soloveitchik, "the Halakhah commands the mourner to undertake a heroic task: to start picking up the debris of his own shattered personality and to reestablish himself as man, restoring lost glory, dignity, and uniqueness."[27]

While a person's emotions are powerful and need expression, humans are capable of controlling them:

> The Halakhah is firmly convinced that man is free and that he is master not only of his deeds but of his emotions as well. The Halakhah holds the view that man's mastery of

---

27. R. Joseph B. Soloveitchik, "*Aninut* and *Avelut*," in *Out of the Whirlwind*, p. 4.

his emotional life is unqualified and that he is capable of changing thought patterns, emotional structures, and experiential motifs within an infinitesimal period of time.

Man, the Halakhah maintains, does not have to wait patiently for one mood to pass and for another to emerge gradually. He disengages himself, quickly and actively, and in a wink replaces a disjunctive frame of mind with a cathartic-redemptive one. Hence, the Halakhah, which showed so much tolerance for the mourner during the stage of *aninut,* and let him float with the tide of black despair, now—forcefully and with a shift of emphasis—commands him that, with interment, the first phase of grief comes abruptly to a close and a second phase—that of *avelut*—begins.[28]

There is a tremendous difference between being depressed and being in a depression. There is often good reason to be depressed. Bad things happen to us; we fear for the present and the future. What healthy person would not be depressed when his or her world suddenly collapses around them? But depression is something unhealthy; it is being trapped in one's black despair, ensnared by the tangle of emotions that paralyze as they undermine. If being depressed must be acknowledged and expressed, overcoming depression must be confronted. Hence the Halakhah insists on the immediate reimposition of obligation in mitzvot.

Kaddish

The ceremonial turning point from *aninut* to *avelut* is the saying of *Kaddish.* Mourners' *Kaddish* is a prayer that simply

---

28. Ibid., pp. 3f.

praises God without making reference to death. Yet it is this characterization of the prayer that makes it appropriate to begin to regain control of one's emotions with its recital.

Praise requires suppression of anger; but more importantly, it demands appreciation of self-worth. To praise God is to be aware that one is so important that God is interested in his or her praise. *Kaddish* is not only a declaration of God's greatness but an expression of our awareness that God takes interest in us and in what we do; our actions and our words have importance because life has importance. To assert that principle, the mourners must put aside their loneliness and despair to search out a community, since *Kaddish* can be said only in the context of a *minyan*.

Interestingly, *Kaddish* at the graveside is the special *Kaddish* said at a *siyyum* celebration. The *siyyum* is the completion of the study of a Talmudic tractate or biblical book, and such an accomplishment merits rejoicing. However, said Rabbi Soloveitchik, quoting his father, the essence of the *siyyum* celebration is not our past accomplishments but the anticipation of beginning a new challenge of learning. On Simhat Torah we do not end the reading of Deuteronomy without beginning immediately the reading of Genesis, and the honor of *Hatan Bereshit* (beginning the reading of the book of Genesis) is higher than that of *Hatan Torah* (completing the book of Deuteronomy).[29] At the *siyyum* we make a declaration *da'atan alakh*, our latent awareness is still committed to our past experience, and *hadran alakh*,

---

29. R. Tzvi Yosef Reichman, *Reshimot Sheurim: Sukka* (New York, 5749 [1989]), p. 299.

we will return to what we have just left. At the graveside we look back to what we have lost and promise to return to our memories. It is also a time for looking forward to new accomplishments and relationships.

"Through the *Kaddish*," writes Rabbi Joseph B. Soloveitchik, "we hurl defiance at death and its fiendish conspiracy against man."

> When the mourner recites: "Glorified and sanctified be the great name . . ." he declares: No matter how powerful death is, notwithstanding the ugly end of man, however terrifying the grave is, however nonsensical and absurd everything appears, no matter how black one's despair is and how nauseating an affair life is, we declare and profess publicly and solemnly that we are not giving up, that we are not surrendering, that we will carry on the work of our ancestors as though nothing has happened, that we will not be satisfied with less than the full realization of the ultimate goal—the establishment of God's kingdom, the resurrection of the dead, and eternal life for man.[30]

While Rabbi Soloveitchik's analysis of *Kaddish* speaks to its philosophical importance in expressing defiance at death's attempt to undermine man as a significant being, it does not explain the hold that saying *Kaddish* has on many, including countless people who do not understand the words they are saying, let alone their philosophical underpinnings. "Much has been said in dispraise of Jews who

---

30. Ibid., p. 5.

obey the rules of the *Kaddish* though otherwise they hardly ever pray at all," writes Milton Himmelfarb.

> The contempt is unwarranted; the *Kaddish* must meet their needs better than anything else in the synagogue. Feelings about death, especially the death of a parent; guilt and anxiety, and the need to relieve them; ritual—all these can be interpreted along conventional Freudian lines and have been. . . . [Saying *Kaddish*] is expiatory, it is almost punitive, and we have been taught that guilt seeks punishment.[31]

The source of this guilt and pain that may overwhelm the mourner which Himmelfarb has intuitively sensed is man's sense of memory. Memory is one of man's great blessings; indeed, it is part of human awareness. But in times of mourning, the gift of memory becomes a curse. We realize the opportunities we forfeited in not appreciating those close to us when they were alive. This awareness of loss and lost opportunities is not a philosophical awareness; it springs up unexpectedly and piercingly, as Rabbi Soloveitchik observes:

> There seems to be a tragic flaw inherent in the nature of man from which no one can escape. The people and things that we love and cherish most are not fully appreciated as long as they are alive and present with us . . .
> Over the course of many years a man becomes accustomed to returning home from his outside affairs; he climbs

---

31. Milton Himmelfarb, "Going to Shul," *Commentary*, April 1966, p. 66.

the few steps before the front door of his house in the same way he has done for years. He rings the bell out of habit and expects to hear, as always, soft steps from the other side of the door. He waits; but the steps never come. He puts his hands in his pocket, pulls out the key and opens the door. Everything is clean and polished as usual. Nevertheless, something has changed. Everything appears to be in exactly the same state and in the same place in which they were before he left his house. Nothing has been moved; only no one is there waiting for him. All around there is peace and quiet which can sometimes be worse than heartrending cries. Mourning engulfs his whole being. . . . The longing for one who has died and is gone forever is worse than death. The soul is overcome and shattered by fierce longing.[32]

Ritual helps us confront and deal with these types of feelings, Himmelfarb reminds us—and our response need not necessarily be philosophic. He continues: "The Jewish rites, the burial, the seven days at home, the *Kaddish* have the advantage of being a tradition, a style. We need assume no responsibility for them, as we would for any personal or private symbolic action, nor can there be any question of their appropriateness."

These observations center on the effect of *Kaddish* on the *mourner*; yet the popular assumption is that its purpose is to bring relief to the *deceased*. This relates to a well-known

---

32. Pinchas H. Peli, *On Repentance in the Thought of Rabbi Joseph B. Soloveitchik* (Jerusalem: Oroth, 1980), pp. 278, 214, 280.

story[33] about the effect of its recitation on the soul of the departed.

Once R. Akiva saw a man who was carrying a heavy load. Questioning him, R. Akiva found that he was a dead man who was punished anew each day by being sent to chop wood for a fire with which he was consumed. He had been a tax collector and was being punished for having been lenient with the rich but oppressive of the poor. He told R. Akiva that he had heard that he would have been released from his punishment if only he had left a son who would stand before the congregation and proclaim either *Barekhu et Hashem ha-mevorakh,* to which the congregation would respond *Barukh Hashem ha-mevorakh le-olam va-ed,* or *Yitgadal ve-yitkadash shemei rabba,* to which the congregation would respond *Yehei shemei rabba mevorakh.*

R. Akiva set out to find the child, had him circumcised, and personally taught him Torah and the order of the prayers. When he was ready, R. Akiva appointed him to lead the congregation in prayer. When the people responded *Yehei shemei rabba* to his *Kaddish,* his father's tortured soul was immediately freed from its punishment. (Interestingly, R. Akiva's actions resulted not only in the redemption of the boy's father but of the community as well. They had failed in their obligation to circumcise and educate the orphaned boy.)

It is the communal responsive declaration of praise that effects redemption of the soul of the deceased. Originally,

---

33. R. Yitzhak ben Moshe mi-Vina, *Or Zaru'a* (Zhitomir ed.), vol. 2, *Hilkhot Shabbat,* paragraph 50, p. 22, among other places.

the mourner would recite *Barekhu* in his capacity as *hazzan* and thereby elicit the congregation's praise of God in response. But not everybody has the ability to act as *hazzan* (or receive one of the few *aliyot* that also have a community response). The early authorities therefore enacted the saying of *Kaddish* after the recitation of the final Psalms in the service, which is outside of the formal prayer service, to provide an opportunity for those who would be excluded from acting as *hazzan* to elicit a community response in praise of God.[34]

Originally, only one person would say *Kaddish* at each opportunity, and the early authorities have well-developed rules for who takes precedence over whom, depending on the mourner's relationship to the deceased. Women have no obligation to pray with a *minyan* in a synagogue; therefore they could not claim a right to be the one to say *Kaddish* there, inasmuch as they would displace a man who has an obligation. But this rule would not apply outside of the synagogue in a private *minyan* where no one else is claiming a right to be the one who says *Kaddish*. Thus Rabbi Yehuda Ashkenazi writes, "Certainly the daughter has no *Kaddish* in the synagogue, but if they wish to form a separate *minyan* for her, they are permitted to do so."[35] Similarly, Rabbi

---

34. Viz. R. Naftali Zvi Roth, "Azkarah ve-Haftarah ve-Kaddish Yatom," *Talpiyot* 7:2–4, Tishrei 5721 [1961], pp. 369–381.

35. R. Yehuda Ashkenazi, *Be'er Heitev*, n. 5, in R. Yisrael Meir Ha-Kohein (known as the Hafetz Hayim *Mishnah Berurah*, vol. 2, sec. 132.

Hayyim Mordecai Margoliyot rules, "If he had only a daughter, she may say *Kaddish*, but only in her house."[36]

Eventually, the pressure of many people wanting to say *Kaddish* forced a new etiquette: all mourners would say *Kaddish* together, and this is the procedure followed in most congregations today. Now that a woman would not displace a man who wanted to be the one to say *Kaddish*, there is no reason for women not to be able to join them in the synagogue, as opposed to being restricted to a private *minyan*. Such a position is neither radical nor innovative. Rabbi Moshe Feinstein notes that "throughout the generations it was customary that at times a poor woman would enter the *bet midrash* to ask for charity, or a woman mourner would enter to say *Kaddish*."[37]

Indeed, allowing women to say *Kaddish* in the synagogue is the position taken by leading Lithuanian *poskim* of the past generation, including Rabbis Hayyim Ozer Grodzinski, Yosef Eliyahu Henkin, and Joseph B. Soloveitchik.[38] Rabbi Soloveitchik adds that there is no problem if she is the sole individual saying *Kaddish*, which is not at all surprising, since in the past she would have been the sole person saying *Kaddish* in a private *minyan*.

---

36. R. Hayyim Mordecai Margoliyot, *Sha'arei Teshuvah*, n. 5, in *Mishnah Berurah*, ibid.

37. R. Moshe Feinstein, *Iggerot Moshe, Orah Hayyim* V:12.

38. See the more extensive discussion in my *Women, Jewish Law and Modernity*.(Hoboken, N.J.: Ktav, 1997), pp. 84–94.

To be sure, few women over the past centuries have chosen to say *Kaddish*, and indeed to this very day there are
various *poskim* who oppose women's saying *Kaddish*, be it
in shul or even in a private *minyan*. Their reasoning has
been, for the most part, that changing the status quo, even
if technically permissible, weakens Jewish tradition. In rejecting this fear, Rabbi Aaron Soloveichik comments that
nowadays, when those outside of the halakhic community
are advocating full equality for men and women in all ritual
matters, if Orthodox rabbis prevent women from saying
Kaddish when there is a possibility for allowing it, the influence of those who are fighting actual halakhic norms will
be strengthened. Prohibiting what is permitted can lead to
permitting what is actually prohibited. He concludes, "It is
therefore forbidden to prevent daughters from saying *Kaddish*."[39]

Leaving the Cemetery

As the mourners are about to leave, the community steps
forward. First they join the mourners in saying *tziduk ha-
din*, the declaration that God is just, repeating in a sense
the mourner's blessing recited at the time of *keriyah* that
God is a *Dayan Emet*, a true judge. They then line up in
two rows facing each other and, as the mourners pass
through them, they recite together the phrase that each will

39. R. Aaron Soloveichik, *Od Yisrael Yosef Beni Hai*, no. 32.

eventually say individually when leaving the *shiva* house. (Ashkenazim say, *Hamakom yinahem et'khem betokh sha'ar avlei Tziyon ve-Yerushalaim,* "May you be comforted among the other mourners of Zion and Jerusalem"; Sephardim say, *Min haShamayim tinuhamu,* "May you be comforted from Heaven"). At this moment of extreme loneliness, the mourners cannot go home without passing through the community. The attendants must be lined up and there must be a *minyan* present; it is the *community* that is offering support, not individual friends. It is the community that is timeless, having lived through and survived centuries of deaths and tragedies. Indeed, the community must be present when the mourners recite *Kaddish,* for it is only within its supportive presence and with its collective response that the mourners may begin to recapture and express their human dignity.

The Meal of Consolation

Avelut begins with burial and the saying of *Kaddish* and soon thereafter continues with the *se'udat havra'a,* the Meal of Consolation (or Recovery) served to the mourners when they return home from the burial. There are various customs concerning the foods served at this meal, but there is one basic halakhah that governs it. *Shulhan Arukh* rules, "The mourner may not eat of his own for the first meal . . . and it is a mitzvah for the neighbors to feed him from theirs so that he not eat from his own."[40] Indeed, the Jerusalem Talmud[41] says, "a curse on the neighbors" if they force the mourners to eat their first meal from their own food.

The logic of this halakhah is clear. In their moment of intense loneliness, it is unthinkable for the mourners to return to an empty house; the community must be there to feed them. The mourners are distraught over their loss and have no interest in eating, hoping to die themselves;[42] their friends are there to tell them that life goes on, that as strange as this may seem to them now, they will want to eat; that as lonely and abandoned as they might feel at the moment, they are part of a community that is there to support and nurture them. Indeed, a curse on the neighbors if they desert the mourners in their hour of need. And just as the community may not abandon the mourners, the mourners may not retreat from the community; they may not reinforce their sense of isolation by eating of their own. They are obligated to reach out to those who are obligated to be there for them. In the Jewish tradition, being comforted is an essential expression of mourning.[43]

Interestingly, the tradition was concerned not only with the mourners and their community of support, but with the overall community dynamics. "Formerly, they used to serve drinks in the house of mourning, the rich in white glass

---

40. *Yoreh De'ah* 378:1.

41. J.T. Moed Katan 3:5.

42. R. Yehoshua Falk Katz, *Perisha* to R. Yaakov ben R. Asher, *Tur* 378:1.

43. Viz. Rashi, Sanhedrin 47b, s.v. *Ho'il.*

vessels and the poor in colored glass. The poor felt shamed, and it was therefore instituted that all should serve drinks in colored glass."[44] Neither the mourners' self-concern nor their friends' concern for them can allow being oblivious to the ethical needs of the community as a whole.

It is not by accident that the wine served at the meal is mentioned explicitly. Wine is traditionally a symbol of joy. "There is no joy except with meat and wine" is the reason both are required for a holiday meal.[45] The *onen* is prohibited from drinking wine, but if the reason were its association with joy, it would be prohibited to the *avel* as well. Rather, it is other dimensions of wine that are involved here.

The first is that wine is the halakhic paradigm of a social drink. *Stam yeinam* (the prohibition to drink wine that was in the possession of gentiles) is, unlike *kashrut* regulations, based on limiting social interaction rather than fear of contamination with nonkosher ingredients. The *onen*'s prohibition reflects, then, his or her estrangement from society, the shattering of one's social self and searing loneliness that accompanies a confrontation with death. The wine served at the Meal of Consolation reflects the *avel*'s reintegration with society and the reconstruction of his or her own shattered personality

The second dimension is that wine is the instrument used to call attention to the fact that an important *berakhah* is

---

44. Moed Katan 27a.
45. *Mishneh Torah, Hilkhot Yom Tov* 6:18.

about to be said. For example, *Kiddush, Havdalah, Sheva Berakhot* are all said over a cup of wine. Originally, there was a series of *Birkat Avelim* (Mourners' Blessings) that were said at the initiation of *avelut* following the burial. This series of blessings were seen as parallel to *Birkat Hatanim*, the *Sheva Berakhot* said in honor of the bride and groom under the *huppah*. For some reason, the former has fallen into disuse while the latter continues to be said to this day. Both were seen as *berakhot* with a social dimension; each series required the presence of a *minyan* and were introduced with a cup of wine. *Birkat Avelim* was said either in a public place where the mourners were served their meal before returning or when they reached home and were about to be served the Meal of Consolation. There were diverse practices concerning *Birkat Avelim*; apparently they could be extended with either a homily or words of comfort, depending on the rhetorical powers of the comforter.[46]

The first blessing praises God: "God, infinitely awe-inspiring in His might and power, Who will resurrect the dead by His word, Whose deeds are great, inscrutable, marvelous, and infinite. Blessed are You, O Lord, Who will resurrect the dead."

The second blessing was to comfort the mourners: "Our brothers, saddened and crushed with guilt, set your minds on this, for it stands forever. It is a path traveled since creation. Many have drunk [of this sorrow] and many will drink it in all ages. Our brethren, may the Lord comfort you. Blessed . . . Who comforts mourners."

---

46. See Ketubot 8b and the summary discussion in *Encyclopedia Talmudit*, vol. 4, s.v. *Birkat Avelim*.

The third blessing was addressed to the comforters who had come to express sympathy for the mourners: "Our brethren, gracious children of gracious fathers, who hold fast to the covenant of our father Abraham, may He Who rewards requite your kindness. Blessed are You . . . Who requites kindness."

The fourth blessing was a prayer: "Lord of the universe, redeem, deliver, rescue, and save Your people Israel from plagues, the sword, robbery, blight, decay, and every worldly calamity. Answer our supplication even before we cry out. Blessed are You . . . Who keeps plagues from us."

Drinking wine has a third dimension to it, one that flows from its social etiquette. Wine is part of controlled drinking of alcohol. To be sure, one can become intoxicated by drinking wine, but its drinking at a formal meal is accompanied by a social etiquette, which implies elements of control, discipline, and dignity. "Once the dead has been buried, one is permitted to eat meat and drink *a small amount* of wine."[47] Initiating *avelut* with wine therefore serves a reminder of a major theme of the whole halakhic mourning experience: expression of emotions tempered with control.

Overturned Beds and Covered Mirrors

Originally, all the beds in a House of Mourning were overturned. Bar Kapparah taught his disciples, "God says, 'I

---

47. *Shulhan Arukh, Yoreh De'ah* 378:8.

have set the likeness of My image in them, and through their sins have I upset it. Let your beds be overturned on account of this."[48] Rabbi Soloveitchik explains:

> The central motif here is that death impinges upon the worth of human dignity and the human divine nature. Man dies deprived of dignity and without his divine humanity. The symbol of humiliated man, of man who goes down in defeat, insult, and shame, is an overturned bed. The bed is a metaphor for the moral integrity of the family (*mittato sheleima*) or the human personality in general (*mitatto porahat ba-avir*).[49]

This custom has long fallen into disuse, since beds are no longer constructed so that they can be easily overturned. Now the covered mirror symbolizes the individual's alienation from his or her human self and the inability to find the divine image that still resides within. Of course, covering the mirrors also represents diverting focus from our everyday needs. It is hard to pass a mirror without taking note of how we look; but during *shiva* the mourners should be concerned with their loss, not their self-image. It should not matter if one's hair is combed just right or if one's clothes are properly pressed, and, indeed, wearing freshly pressed clothes and bathing are prohibited to the mourners.

---

48. Moed Katan 15a–b.
49. R. Joseph B. Soloveitck, "Individual and Historical Mourning," in *Out of the Whirlwind*, p. 29.

The *Shiva* Call

A Silent Entrance

The importance of the *shiva* call as a central component
of the mourning experience is expressed in a commentary to one of the verses in the twenty-fourth chapter
of Ezekiel, the biblical section from which the Talmud[50]
learns many of the details of halakhic mourning practices.
The people are warned that catastrophe is coming, but, as
Rashi points out (v. 22), they will not be able to observe
avelut (formal mourning), since there will be no comforters.
Everyone will be bereaved and there can be no *avelut* without comforters. *Nihum avelim* (comforting the mourners)
is an essential component of Jewish mourning. One mourns
as part of a community, not in isolation.

The *shiva* call—the primary vehicle for offering formal
comfort and consolation—has three components: one's entrance, conversation with the mourners, and departure. The
first and last have a formal component, but the discussion
is more complex and carries with it greater possibility of
inappropriate action.

---

50. Moed Katan 15.

One must enter the unlocked *shiva* house silently without announcement, sit quietly with the mourners, and remain silent until the mourners have opened the conversation. Neither mourner nor comforter formally greet one another, an etiquette the Talmud adopts from God's instruction to Ezekiel (24:17), "Grieve and be silent."

This imposed silence until recognized by the mourners accomplishes a number of goals. First, it salvages some of the privacy forfeited by the mourners in the open environment of people simply entering at will. Second, it protects the comforter from the fear of having nothing to say. True, the visitor wants to communicate concern and an offer to help. That has already been expressed by simply entering and sitting quietly. Indeed, if not for this rule, sensitive people might be afraid to pay a *shiva* call. What should they say when there is nothing to say! Thus the tradition assures everyone that it is the situation and not their inadequacies that leaves them speechless. No one need fear coming to offer condolences. Third, those people who are sure that they really do have a meaningful message are forced to hesitate before sharing their self-assured problem-solving thoughts.

That such hesitation is in order is in some ways the basic theme of the Book of Job. The bulk of the book is a transcript of the *shiva* visit paid by Job's friends. Each offers a philosophic discourse on the reason for Job's suffering and the proper response he should adopt. If we hadn't read the opening chapter of the book, we would not have known that they were all wrong. They had no understanding of why Job was stricken and no justification in offering the advice they did. Alas, many people who pay contemporary *shiva* calls do not take into account that they too had not read the chapter that explains how the world works. A silent entrance gives them pause to consider that fact.

Talmudic Transcripts

It's hard to say what constitutes appropriate discourse for a *shiva* visit, but it is instructive to listen in as the Talmud provides minutes of various inappropriate condolence calls. It should not surprise us that the Talmud records less-than-ideal rabbinic responses. The Rabbis of the Talmudic period were the towers of our tradition; all that we do religiously stands on their shoulders. In showing them to have human frailties, the Talmud does not diminish them; it humbles us. If these giants could not always find the right word, we should not be so sure of our own abilities to comfort and explain.

One such Talmudic anecdote[51] concerns Ulla, the fourth-century scholar who had at times traveled to Babylonia. The daughter of Rav Shmuel bar Yehuda had died and the Rabbis suggested that Ulla join them to comfort him. He refused. "What use do I have with these Babylonian comforters," he said. "They console by saying 'What can be done?'" He felt that such consolation was akin to blas-

---

51. Bava Kamma 38a–b.

phemy, because it suggested that they would change God's judgment if but they could.

Ulla felt that he had a more appropriate message of consolation to deliver, so he went by himself. The Jews were not allowed to wage war against Moab, he said, because Ruth (from whom King David descended) and Nama Ha-Ammonite (King Solomon's wife and mother of Rahavam) were to descend from them. If the daughter of Rav Shmuel bar Yehuda were righteous and worthy of having such worthy descendants, he explained, she surely would have been spared. God is indeed just.

In commenting on Ulla's message, Rabbi Shlomo Luria[52] notes that "What can one do?" is hardly blasphemy. It is nothing more than an expression of the fact that crying and excessive mourning will not bring back the deceased—something King David himself said when his baby son died: "While the child was yet alive, I fasted and wept: for I said, Who can tell whether God will be gracious to me, that the child may live? But now he is dead, why should I fast? Can I bring him back again?" (2 Sam 12:22–23). Moreover, R. Luria added, Ulla's comments are hurtful—and incorrect. It is often the case that righteous children die even though they were indeed worthy to have good things emerge from them. Better to comfort the mourners with talk of praise for the deceased.

R. Luria makes important points in his comments. It is not simply that Ulla was wrong; it is that the purpose of

---

52. R. Shlomo Luria, *Yam Shel Shlomo*, no. 10.

condolences is not to present philosophical positions but to comfort the mourners. Moreover, he says, the fact that neither Rif nor the Rosh quote Ulla's position in their halakhic summaries indicates that they reject it. The correct way to comfort mourners is to actually comfort them, not confront or lecture them.

This latter point was made strongly in an anecdote[53] concerning the death of the child of Rabbi Yohanan ben Zakai. The father was inconsolable and his students came to comfort him.

> Rabbi Eliezer said, Adam had a son who died, and he accepted consolations. You too should accept consolations! He replied, Is it not enough that I must suffer from my own loss; must you also remind me of Adam's loss?!
>
> Rabbi Yehoshia said, Job had sons and daughters who all died in one day, and he accepted consolations. You too should accept consolations! He replied, Is it not enough that I must suffer from my own loss; must you also remind me of Job's loss?!
>
> Rabbi Yossi said, Aaron had two sons who both died in one day, and he accepted consolations. You too should accept consolations! He replied, Is it not enough that I must suffer from my own loss; must you also remind me of Aaron's loss?!
>
> Rabbi Shimon said, King David had a son who died, and he accepted consolations. You too should accept consolations! He replied, Is it not enough that I must suffer from my own loss; must you also remind me of King David's loss?!

---

53. *Avot deRabbi Natan*, version 1, chap. 14, abridged slightly here.

It is not surprising that none of these rabbis was able to comfort the father. What difference does it make if others could overcome their grief or if the "right thing to do" is to be consoled? They were properly rebuffed. Finally, Rabbi Elazar ben Arakh said: You, Rebbe, had a son. He learned Torah, Prophets, the Writings, Mishnah, halakhot and aggadot; he died free of sin. You should be consoled as you returned whole that which was given to you for safekeeping.

Here was consolation directed to the father: You did well in raising him, he said. Nothing more could be expected of you. Your son was a wonderful person; he died free of sin. No wonder the father responded: My son, you have consoled me the way people are indeed consoled.

Another example[54] of inappropriate comfort is found in explaining another's suffering. A person who is suffering, we are told there, should scrutinize his actions to see if he is being punished for any sin. If he is sinless, perhaps he is being punished for neglecting the study of Torah. But if that too does not ring true, then it must be *yissurin shel ahavah*, "afflictions of love." Rashi explains that God causes the guiltless to suffer in this world so that they might reap even greater rewards in the next. Somehow, God must "justify" the rewards to be received. As Rava said in the name of Sehora quoting R. Huna, God crushes with sufferings all those in whom He takes delight. And if the sufferer accepts these sufferings with love, his rewards will include seeing his children live a long life and having his Torah studies

---

54. Berakhot 5a–b.

endure. An innocent righteous person should apparently be comforted by the fact that he is one in whom God takes delight.

Maimonides[55] argued that the concept of *yissurin shel ahavah* is not to be found in the Torah. It would seem that it is first associated with R. Yohanan, the second-generation Palestinian Talmudic scholar who eventually became the head of the yeshivah in Tiberius. He himself was one of those pious Jews who had led a hard life. Orphaned at birth, he saw his family fortune go from riches to rags, and eventually he buried each of his ten sons. R. Yaakov bar Iddi and R. Aha bar Hanina, we are told, argued whether *yissurin shel ahavah* could encompass even those sufferings which cause one to neglect prayer or the study of Torah. But R. Hiyya bar Abba said in the name of R. Yohanan that even in such cases one can explain away the undeserved pain by attributing it to *yissurin shel ahavah*.

It is hard to argue with such a neat explanation. After all, who can really understand why God does what He does. But the Gemara, with what seems to be a touch of irony, proceeds to show that R. Yohanan's all-encompassing explanation sounds better in the abstract than in its application to specific individuals:

A Tanna appears to recite a *beraita* before R. Yohanan: "Whoever occupies himself with the Torah or with kindnesses toward others, or goes through the trauma of burying his children, is forgiven all his sins." R. Yohanan quickly

---

55. Maimonides, *Guide for the Perplexed*, III:17.

accepts the first two, but the third just does not sit well with him. Somehow, it does not make sense to him to see such positive consequences from the death of one's child that way. In fact, R. Yohanan was wont to say that having open and embarrassing bodily plagues or being childless could not possibly be *yissurin shel ahavah.*

The Gemara is a bit uneasy with R. Yohanan's last statement. Could "childless" mean having had children and losing them, it asks. But R. Yohanan used to say, "This is the bone of my tenth son!" (It seems that R. Yohanan used to carry around some sort of bone of his tenth deceased son and bring it to *shiva* calls. "Look," he would tell the mourner, "I've had such troubles and accept them with love; certainly you can be reconciled to your troubles.") Hence R. Yohanan's *bon mot* regarding plagues and childlessness must refer to a person who never had children, concludes the Gemara, not one who lost his children. The latter suffering might well be *yissurin shel ahavah.*

It is not surprising that R. Yohanan was hesitant to accept the full *beraita* recited before him. On another occasion[56] he had quoted R. Simeon bar Yohai's maxim that "childlessness must be the result of sin." But, says the Gemara there, R. Yohanan used to go around showing the bone of his tenth (and last) son; certainly he did not consider himself a sinner! Ah, the Gemara concludes, he was only quoting R. Simeon bar Yohai, not agreeing with him.

It is not clear whether R. Yohanan's condolences were effective. He knew that when paying a *shiva* call one could

---

56. Bava Batra 116a.

not intrude with explanations or continue talking if the mourner had heard enough, and he was sensitive to the fact that the best-intentioned remark could be misunderstood.[57] But he could not put his sons' deaths (or their artifacts) behind him and kept explaining his and others' sufferings as *yissurin shel ahavah*. Perhaps he was right; we shall not know until we get to the next world. One senses, though, that it was easier for R. Yohanan to offer this explanation of a child's death to others than to accept it when it was presented to him.

Our uneasiness with R. Yohanan's pat explanation of the afflictions of innocent people should not be confused with the simple acceptance of its alternative. When R. Yohanan's student R. Ami proclaimed (B. *Shabbat* 55a-b) that there is neither death nor suffering without sin, no less than the heavenly angels responded with amazement. R. Ami's explanation is rejected—*tiyuvta d'Rav Ami tiyuvta*—because, after all, the rabbis knew that people had died and suffered without sinning. But if R. Ami is wrong, R. Yohanan may be right. Perhaps. It's just that in explaining why bad things happen to good people, one should have the good sense to realize that explanations that sound good to one person may not be so comforting when offered to others. It is best to be silent when entering the *shiva* house. Indeed, the Talmud tells us,[58] "Our Rabbis taught: 'Do not wrong one another' (Lev. 25:17) refers to verbal wrongs (*ona'at devarim*). . . . If

---

57. Moed Katan 27b.
58. Bava Metzi'a 58b.

a person is visited by suffering, afflicted with disease, or has buried his children, one must not speak to him as his companions spoke to Job, 'What innocent man ever perished? Where have the upright been destroyed?' (Job 4:7)."

Of course, as a matter of abstract philosophy, we believe that there *is* meaning to our suffering, that "God saw *all things* that He had made and, behold, it was very good" (Gen. 1:31). But the question is whether such a message can be heard by the mourner. Writes Rabbi Joseph B. Soloveitchik:

> Can such a metaphysic bring solace and comfort to modern man who finds himself in crisis, facing the monstrosity of evil, and to whom existence and absurdity appear to be bound up inextricably together? Is there in the transcendental and universal message a potential of remedial energy to be utilized by the rabbi who comes, like Zofar, Bildad, and Eliphaz, the three friends of Job, to share the burden and to comfort his congregant in distress? We know that the friends of Job were not that successful in convincing Job about the nonexistence of evil. Can a rabbi be more successful? Can he succeed where the biblical friends of Job failed miserably? . . . I can state with all candor that I personally have not been too successful in my attempts to spell out this metaphysic in terms meaningful to the distraught individual who floats aimlessly in all-encompassing blackness, like a withered leaf on a dark autumnal night tossed by wind and rain. I tried but failed, I think, miserably, like the friends of Job[59]

59. R. Joseph B. Soloveitchik, "A Halakhic Approach to Suffering," in *Out of the Whirlwind,"* pp. 99f.

Conversation in the Shiva *House*

What, then, is the proper conversation that should take place during a *shiva* visit? One positive example was that of Rabbi Elazar ben Arakh quoted above. "People are indeed consoled" when we praise the deceased and the mourner's life with him or her. We bring our good memories, not our philosophy, to the *shiva* house and we are generous when we share them. There is no script that can be written for the discussion that follows the mourners' acknowledgement of the visitor's presence; one can only respond humbly in support of the mourners. Indeed, the key is "responding" and not imposing. There is a need to listen to the mourner and respond to his or her comments. Open-ended questions about the deceased are in order, but one also has to be sensitive to lack of response.

We might well note yet another instructive anecdote[60] regarding paying a *shiva* call to one who has buried his child. R. Hiyya bar Abba's son had died, and Resh Lakish went to comfort him accompanied by his *meturgaman* (interpreter or translator), Yehuda ben Nahmani. Instructed by Resh Lakish to say something appropriate, Yehuda ben Nahmani said, "'And the Lord saw and spurned, because of the provoking of His sons and daughters' (Deut 32:19)—in a generation in which fathers spurn God, He is angry, and their sons and daughters die when they are young." Startled by the suggestion that appropriate com-

---

60. Ketubot 8b.

forting in such a case might include telling the father that the son had died in punishment for the former's sins, the Gemara asks, "He came to comfort and he grieved him?!"

Attempting to reframe these hurtful words, the Gemara then offers the explanation that Yehuda ben Nahmani was not accusing R. Hiyya of sinning, but was rather saying that he was important enough to be held responsible for the shortcomings of the generation. Yet not every hurtful word can be withdrawn retroactively. It is interesting to note a contemporary reaction to this story. The father of a deceased eight-year-old girl would relate this Talmudic anecdote to those who were paying him a *shiva* call and ask: "How do you understand this Gemara? Is there comfort in losing a little girl for whatever transcendent reason?" The dead girl's grandparent added, "The question hung in the air like a heavy, dark cloud. I do not recall any answers that dispelled that cloud."[61]

One must come to comfort the mourners and not grieve them.

Leaving the Shiva House

The *shiva* visit commences with silence because, as we said, there is really nothing meaningful to be said other than that the visitor is there to support the mourner, and that has been "said" by his or her entering the room and sitting

---

61. Seryl Sander, *Times of Challenge* (Brooklyn, NY: Mesorah Publications, 1988), pp. 42f.

down. When one has nothing meaningful to say, it is best to say nothing.

When it is time to leave, the comforter recites what might seem to be a trite phrase. Ashkenazim say, *Hamakom yinahem etkhem betokh sha'ar avlei Tziyon ve-Yerushalaim,* "May you be comforted among the other mourners of Zion and Jerusalem"; Sephardim say, *Min haShamayim tinahamu,* "May you be comforted from Heaven." How can a phrase-turned-cliché by its constant repetition over and over throughout the week have meaning?

But the repetitive rendition of the canonical words of comfort actually complements the silent entry. As an individual, the comforter really has nothing to say. How can he or she pretend to have an answer that makes sense? How can people who are not crushed personally by death have the gall to say that things will be okay? Individuals have no such right, but the community does. It is the community that can offer support, because it is the community that has survived endless assaults on its hopes and dreams. In exiting, the comforter tells the mourner to pay attention to the fact that everyone is saying the same phrase. It is the community's message.

The End of Shiva

Shiva begins with a courageous statement that life still has meaning and that the black despair that an encounter with death generates can be overcome. The community plays an important part in maintaining a structure and reservoir of support. But ending *shiva* also requires a courageous attitude as the mourners realize that those who were ever-present now proceed to go on their way.

In theory, *shiva* ends right after the beginning of the seventh day, since "part" of the day is considered a full day. Yet the community is involved one final time. *Shiva* actually ends "when the comforters have departed from the mourner."[62] Being able to be comforted is an essential component of mourning. When the comforters leave, *shiva* must end. (Of course, the mourners are not "hostage" to the comforters; they rise when the community members *should* have come, that is, at the end of the community morning services.)

In some communities the comforters add two verses after they tell the mourners to rise: "No more shall your sun set; nor shall the moon withdraw itself; for the Lord shall be your everlasting light, and the days of your mourning shall be ended" (Isaiah 60:20) followed by "As one whom his mother comforts, so will I comfort you; and you shall be comforted in Jerusalem" (Isaiah 66:13). The mourners rise, put on their shoes, and deliberately leave the house to return to the outside world.

---

62. *Shulhan Arukh, Yoreh De'ah* 395:1

"Those Who Bury Their Children"

Unmitigated Tragedy

We had mentioned earlier the Talmudic requirement that mourners who inherit from their deceased parent must say the *berakhah* of *Sheheheyanu* along with that of *Dayan Emet*. While the circumstances through which the inheritance was acquired were painful and surely unwanted, the positive aspect of the bequest cannot be denied. But, says Rabbi Akiva Eiger,[63] if parents inherit from the death of their child, *Sheheheyanu* is not said, because the death of one's child is a complete and unmitigated tragedy. There is nothing positive hidden in it.

"*Kover et banav*, those who bury their children are forgiven all their sins," says the Talmud.[64] This is not to say that the children died because of their parents' sins. "The person who sins, he alone shall die. A child shall not share the burden of a parent's guilt, nor shall a parent share the

---

63. Gloss to *Shulhan Arukh, Orah Hayyim* 223:2.
64. Berakhot 5b.

burden of a child's guilt; the righteousness of the righteous shall be accounted to him alone, and the wickedness of the wicked shall be accounted to him alone" (Ezekiel 18:20). Rather, it means that any punishment that might eventually be inflicted upon a person for his or her sins pales in comparison with the pain of losing a child. A person who experiences such pain is crushed and hence is "immune" from further punishment. One simply can't hold anything against them. "They are forgiven all their sins."

Of course, there are those who have searched for an explanation of this tragedy, just as they have searched out other theodicies to justify God's actions. We earlier encountered Ulla's explanation that children die because God had determined that nothing good will come from them, and we noted Rabbi Shlomo Luria's condemnation of such an explanation as hurtful and prohibited. It would not be hard to compile a list of other explanations offered over the years. We shall not rehearse them here, because in the end they are all unsatisfying.

Indeed, that is one of the main points of the book of Job. If we had not read the first chapter, we might have thought that some or all the explanations offered by Job's friends for his misfortune, which included burying his children, were correct. The first chapter, then, is perhaps the most important of all those of the book. Having read the introduction to Job, we know that as good as those theories for his suffering might sound, they were not correct. But we do not get to read the "introductory chapter" of life to learn which theories are correct and which are not. If silence is in general the correct posture in paying a *shiva* call, it is certainly appropriate for those who would comfort those who have buried their children.

A Contrast in Mourning

Burying a child is not only a reversal of the natural ideal, according to which children bury their parents after 120 years. "The death of a parent is not as devastating psychologically as is the death of a child," writes Rabbi Joseph B. Soloveitchik.

> Parents who have lost a child will never forget their grief. Their distress is endless; nothing can offer them solace. A son and a daughter, on the other hand, can usually get past the death of the parent. And yet the Halakhah has decreed thirty days' mourning for a child and twelve months of mourning for parents.[65]

The issue of the disparate periods of mourning can be understood when one appreciates that *kavod horim* (respect and honor for parents) is a requirement separate from *kevod ha-beriyot* (the respect and honor due all human beings just by virtue of their having been created in the image of God). Parents deserve an additional measure of respect simply by virtue of their part in the creation of the individual. True,

---

65. R. Joseph B. Soloveitchik, "Abraham Mourns Sarah," in *Out of the Whirlwind*, p. 33.

not every parent earns additional respect by their everyday behavior. Yet *hakarat ha-tov* (expressing gratitude) demands it. There is no halakhic obligation to love one's child; it comes naturally. But there is a commandment to honor one's parents, and one actualization of that is the extended mourning period for parents that does not apply to any other relative.

In addition, notes Rabbi Soloveitchik:

Apparently the Halakhah is guided not by psychological, emotional reality but by concerns about the *Masorah*, the Tradition. A parent dies—the mourning is great. Why? The parent was the person who acquainted me with the *Masorah*. My belonging to the covenantal community is his or her accomplishment—no one else taught me. Hence the death of a person who extended the chain of tradition to an individual must precipitate greater formalized mourning than the death of a child to whom one does not owe any debt of gratitude as far as the *Masorah* is concerned.[66]

The Unmourned Child

It is troubling to many that the death of a *nefel* (a baby who died within thirty days of birth) or a miscarried fetus carries with it no formal mourning, In these cases the parents are apparently deprived of the whole therapeutic mourning process available to all other mourners. To be sure, there is no denying that such a death triggers many of the same

---

66. Ibid.

reactions as does the death of any relative. And, indeed, the absence of formal mourning is meant not to deny comfort and support but to protect the boundaries of human status.

Boundaries are an integral component of the Halakhah's concept of holiness. Time is an uninterrupted continuum in which one instant is indistinguishable from the next. Yet Shabbat begins at a particular point. One second before, striking a match lights up a room; a second after, the same act desecrates the holiness of the day. One can walk out of one's town on Shabbat and, in one step that is indistinguishable from the one before it, violate the holiness of the day by crossing the limits of travel outside one's city that is permitted on Shabbat. Similarly, the holiness of the Temple precincts and Jerusalem are defined according to their respective boundaries.

Human life is a continuum from the moment of conception to the moment of death (the exact time of which is itself a subject of debate). But only at a specific moment—"when its head emerges"—will the Halakhah forbid it to be killed to save the mother. So, too, there is a moment when the Halakhah assumes that the newborn is viable: the end of the thirtieth day after birth. Before that the death cannot be mourned as the passing of a full-fledged human.

A *shiva* call takes precedence over a *bikkur holim* visit to a sick individual, because the latter act is a *hesed* (an expression of kindness) for only the sick person whereas the former is a *hesed* for both the mourner and the deceased. A *nefel*—and certainly a miscarried fetus—does not have full human status and so cannot be mourned formally. But the parents have not forfeited their right to the *hesed* that is due a suffering person. They are entitled to the same attention and support, albeit under the rubric of *bikkur holim* (visiting the sick) and not *nihum avelim* (comforting the mourners).

Bikkur Holim

Kibbud (honor) requires formalism; we show respect by doing something that, in a sense, is illogical. For example, there is no real connection between standing up and showing respect; it is simply a formal gesture. We stand because there is no rational reason to do so other than to show respect. *Kibbud* requires well-acknowledged rules of behavior. *Hesed*, however, requires "only" compassion and its expression.

The respect that the community must pay a deceased person is done at the expense, so to speak, of the mourners' privacy. (For example, the door to the *shiva* house is unlocked and people enter unannounced and uninvited.) However, in the case of a miscarriage or the death of a *nefel*, the level of public awareness varies with each family, and the extent of public *bikkur holim* should reflect these differences. The same response will generally not do for both the case of an early miscarriage and that of a child who dies after twenty days in the intensive care unit following birth.

On a personal level, the most important reaction is an expression of concern. "How can I help you?" is usually the most appropriate response. On a communal level, it is usually important to approach the mourner with a suggestion before implementing it. Here, too, options depend on what the concerned individuals would find appropriate. Some might find solace in a contribution to some charity; others might prefer a Torah class attended by friends; still others might find meaning in simply joining a *bikkur holim* group. The key is responding and not abandoning the people in pain.

Here too the Talmud provides negative examples. After introducing R. Yohanan's notion of *yissurin shel ahavah* (the idea that God plagues those whom He loves so that He can reward them later), the Gemara[67] goes on to relate three anecdotes of *bikkur holim*.

Recall that that R. Hiyyah bar Abba had quoted R. Yohanan to the effect that one can explain all sorts of undeserved pain by appealing to *yissurin shel ahavah*. In our first scene, R. Hiyyah bar Abba fell sick and R. Yohanan comes to him to raise his spirits. He asked: "Are your sufferings dear to you?" After all, R. Hiyyah bar Abba was certainly a pious man and so his sickness must be *yissurin shel ahavah* with many rewards yet to be reaped. "Keep them," R. Hiyyah tells R. Yohanan; "I want neither the sufferings nor their rewards." So R. Yohanan cured him.

Soon after, R. Yohanan himself was taken ill and his student, R. Hanina, came to visit. What better cheer could he bring than his mentor's greeting, "Are your sufferings dear

---

67. Berakhot 5b.

to you?" "No," answers R. Yohanan, "I want neither them nor their rewards." So R. Hanina cured him. Now, queries the Gemara, is it not strange that R. Yohanan didn't just cure himself; after all, he was able to cure R. Hiyyah bar Abba. The answer is: A prisoner cannot release himself from his dungeon. And it is a poignant reply, for, as we immediately see, R. Yohanan cannot free himself from his approach to suffering, despite his uneasiness in having others apply it to him.

In the third scene, R. Eleazar is sick and R. Yohanan, now healthy, comes to visit him. The room is dark, but R. Yohanan's beauty fills it with light. R. Eleazar starts to weep. With what must be a warm smile, the Gemara relates their conversation: Why are you crying? asks R. Yohanan."Is it because you did not learn enough Torah? Well, it's the effort that counts! Is it because of your poverty? Don't you realize that it's the next world that's important! Is it because of children? How could *you* cry about that; here is the bone of my tenth son! In response to such sympathy R. Eleazar retorts, I'm crying because such a beautiful person like you will eventually become dust! Now that, says R. Yohanan, is something to cry about! So they both wept. Then R. Yohanan, slipping right into his old patterns, asks: "Are your sufferings dear to you?" By this time we (if not R. Yohanan) know the answer: "I want neither them nor their rewards." So R. Yohanan cured him. One cannot miss the tongue-in-cheek character of this transcript.

It sometimes startles us to see how often the Rabbis were willing to take up the problem of how difficult it is to properly comfort others and how easy it is for even saintly men to err. Avot d'Rabbi Natan[68] relates that when R. Simeon ben Yohai was visiting the sick, he once met a man who was swollen and afflicted with intestinal disease. The man was cursing God, and R. Simeon reprimanded him, "Worthless one! You should be praying for mercy for yourself; but instead you utter blasphemies!" The other said to him, "May the Holy One, blessed be He, remove [these sufferings] from me and lay them on you!"

Most instructively, R. Simeon was not offended by this reaction. Instead he took it as a proper reprimand for his actions. He said, "Justly has the Holy One, blessed be He, dealt with me, since I neglected the study of Torah and occupied myself with idle matters." The "idle matters" were obviously not the mitzvah of visiting the sick; it was rather his insensitivity in addressing the suffering person.

---

68. 41:1

Shabbat and Holiday Mourning

Shabbat Mourning

To the public eye, it seems that mourning is suspended on Shabbat. The mourners rise from their low stools, change their ripped clothes, and leave their homes to go to the synagogue. Yet, halakhically *shiva* is not interrupted by the Sabbath; rather, it is turned inward. The mourners must maintain a private regimen of *devarim she-be-tzina*—things that are hidden in privacy and that are known only to them and those who know them most intimately. The mourners are constrained from bathing, having marital relations, studying Torah—prohibitions whose observance is hidden from public view. Understanding this turn in mourning observance requires an appreciation of both the dynamics of Shabbat observance and the essential value of privacy for the human personality.

The importance of privacy flows from the fact that man was created in God's image:

> As God reveals and conceals, so man discloses and withholds. As concealment is an aspect of divine privacy, so is

it the expression of human privacy: the desire to remain unknown, puzzling, enigmatic, a mystery. . . . For both God and man, therefore, in that they share the character of personality, there must be a tension and balance between privacy and communication, between concealment and disclosure, between self-revelation and self-restraint.

This sense of privacy may be referred to as the ethical quality of *tzeniut* . . . [a term which] comprehends respect for the inviolability of the personal privacy of the individual, whether oneself or another, which is another way of saying respect for the integrity of the self. . . . But privacy is more than a legal right; there is also a moral duty for man to protect his own privacy.[69]

At first glance, it seems that *shiva* is but an assault on the individual's privacy. The mourners' clothes are ripped, exposing their torn heart for all to see. Their front door is unlocked and the boundary of their "space," which is generally protected, is violated by all who would enter. But all this is done to protect them. Rosh (R. Asher ben Yechiel) portrayed mourners as "wanting to be alone in a place of sorrow and darkness in order to be involved in their sorrow."[70] Retreating into themselves would deny them the comfort that comes with being part of a living community which collectively provides comfort and succor.

Yet the tradition protects the private moment too. For example, all may enter the *shiva* house unannounced, but

---

69. R. Norman Lamm "The Fourth Amendment and the Halachah," *Judaism*, 16(3), [1967], pp. 300–312

70. *Piskei HaRosh, Sukka*, chap. 2, no. 7.

none may talk to the mourners until they first address the would-be comforters—there is a limit on how much one can impose oneself on the mourners. Shabbat also protects the mourners' privacy.

We generally think of the prohibitions of Shabbat as testimony to God as Creator. We all create, so to speak, but on Shabbat we hold back to recognize the Ultimate Creator. Hence we refrain from creating a spark or planting a seed. Yet how can we understand that carrying objects about is permitted on Shabbat within one's private domain but forbidden if it crosses the perimeter separating private from public?

The answer is that boundaries relate to another theme of Shabbat: the protection of our human standing and the notion of privacy which is integral to it. Animals recognize only practical territorial boundaries; humans have an awareness of subtle boundaries that signify a private domain. The prohibition of carrying is but a forced awareness of public and private spaces. (An *eruv*, which allows for carrying in the community's domain, does not blur the awareness of boundaries but rather sets new physical ones.) On Shabbat, mourners carve out a private space for themselves to mourn privately without masses of people surrounding them.

Shabbat does not represent a suspension of mourning but a shift in the aspect of the human personality to which it speaks. Paradoxically, in real life the public and private aspects of mourning are experienced simultaneously within the same individual. But while contradictory feelings can be felt coincidentally—such is the puzzling "illogical" fact—

they cannot be expressed at the same time. Nevertheless, each is an integral and indispensable part of the total mourning experience, and the halakhah therefore gives each its separate expression.

This is neither a suspension of *shiva* nor a move to another "stage" in the mourning process—witness the fact that Shabbat falls randomly in the week-long *shiva* period. It complements, rather than contradicts, the weekday *shiva* experience. Maimonides[71] indicates that Moses instituted the seven-day period for both mourning and feasting the bridal couple but doesn't explain the significance of seven days. A simple explanation is that a seven-day span guarantees that Shabbat will be part of the normative *shiva* experience, ensuring that the private dimension of mourning will find expression.

Holiday Mourning

Shabbat and holiday mourning have very different dynamics. Shabbat, as we saw, is an integral part of the *shiva* experience; the private regimen of *devarim she-be-tzina* is counted as part of the *shiva* period. On the other hand, if a holiday begins in the middle of *shiva*, both the public and private dimensions of the mourning period come to an end. If burial occurs on the intermediate days of the holiday,

---

71. *Mishneh Torah, Hilkhot Avelut* 1:1.

even though the *devarim she-be-tzina* restrictions are in effect, they are not recognized as part of *shiva*, which begins only when the holiday ends.

The incompatibility of holiday and *shiva* observance flows from the special requirements in fulfilling these two mitzvot. In general, fulfilling a particular mitzvah—*kiyyum ha-mitzvah*—requires only performing a particular act, a *ma'aseh mitzvah*. Thus, for example, one fulfills one's obligation to eat matzah on Passover eve simply by consciously eating the matzah; one's internal thoughts and feelings are not crucial for the *kiyyum ha-mitzvah* But, insists Rabbi Soloveitchik, the *kiyyum ha-mitzvah* for both mourning and festival observance is the maintenance of an internal state of sorrow or joy, respectively.

> [Mourning] is an inner experience of black despair, of complete existential failure, of the absurdity of being. It is a grisly experience which overwhelms man, which shatters his faith and exposes his I-awareness as a delusion. Similarly the precept of *simhat yom tov* (to rejoice on a holiday) includes not only ceremonial actions, but a genuine experience of joy as well. When the Torah decreed "*Ve-samahta be-hageha*, And you shall rejoice in your feast," it referred, not to merrymaking and entertaining, to artificial gaiety or some sort of shallow hilarity, but to an all-penetrating depth-experience of spiritual joy, serenity, and peace of mind deriving from faith and the awareness of God's presence.[72]

---

72. R. Joseph B. Soloveitchik, "Catharsis," *Tradition*, 17:2 (Spring 1978), pp. 48f.

As these two internal states are by definition mutually exclusive, there is no way of observing both mitzvo*t* at the same time.

Shabbat, unlike a holiday, carries with it no obligation of *simha* (the feeling of joy required on the holidays). Shabbat demands *kibbud* (showing respect for the day of Shabbat). This formal external demeanor is not incompatible with mourning, and observing Shabbat therefore does not contradict the possibility of *shiva*.

If a death occurs during the intermediate days of a holiday, the body is buried but *shiva* (which normally begins immediately after burial) starts only when the festival period is over. Yet the mourner is bound by the laws of private mourning until the end of the holiday, when *shiva* begins. Unlike the private mourning of a Shabbat within *shiva*, which is counted as an integral part of the total *shiva* experience, this very same private mourning during the festival is not. It is, however, counted as part of *sheloshim*, the thirty-day mourning period, which demands only external acts of *kibbud* to honor the deceased and is not in conflict with the dynamics of *simha*.

These prohibitions of private mourning—*devarim she-be-tzina*—that are in effect on the holiday even though *shiva* has not begun are, in a sense, a "lingering *aninut*." Bathing, marital relations, and studying Torah reflect, respectively, a concern for one's body, the intensity of interpersonal relations, and the transcendent value of Torah. They are regularly all prohibited during *aninut*, before *shiva* begins. *Aninut* is an expression of *kibbud ha-met*, the need to show respect for the dead, while engaging in these activities "as one's dead lies before him" is, in a way, a desecration of the dead. Thus these prohibitions go into effect during *aninut* even on Shabbat, and they continue throughout the holiday, even though *shiva* cannot yet begin. The private mourning of a regular Shabbat reflects the mourners' need to maintain a distance from their community. This same private mourning on a holiday reflects the struggle of maintaining a distance between two contradictory obligatory internal dynamics while being unable to shake off the persistent black despair initiated by a confrontation with death.

When *simha* is but a formal external observance, it is consistent with *shiva*. For example, there is a halakhic obligation to rejoice formally on Purim by attending a festive holiday meal, but there is no requirement to maintain an internal sense of happiness. Thus, while public mourning must "retreat" on Purim to allow for the expression of "formal *simha*," the internal dynamics are compatible with *avelut*. Hence the private mourning which remains obligatory on Purim is considered part of *shiva*, which then continues to its conclusion after the holiday.

Halakhically, a bride and groom enjoy a seven-day period of rejoicing following their wedding. This week is a "personal holiday" for the couple and is therefore (like biblical holidays) incompatible with public mourning, which may begin only when the week of rejoicing ends. As with a communal holiday, private mourning by a bride or groom begins immediately, but this private mourning is not considered part of either *shiva* or *sheloshim*.

The rationale for excluding this private mourning from the *sheloshim* count as well is based on the "status" of the newly married couple. The bride and groom are considered royalty within Halakhah, and therefore, like the national sovereign, they stand apart from the community. The king stands apart from his subjects both throughout his reign in general and in mourning in particular. When the people come to bring him the funeral meal, they sit on the ground and he, unlike a "common" mourner, sits on a couch.

In comparing the new couple's status to that of royalty, Halakhah grants integrity to the necessity of their removing themselves from the community to create a new mini-community that will transcend their own individual identities. However, mourning done completely apart from the community lacks an element of integrity and hence cannot be considered part of either *shiva* or *sheloshim*.

Mourning after Delayed Notifications

The relative significance of the public versus private aspects of mourning is expressed in the resolution of an interesting question: Can *shiva* begin on Shabbat? It is rare for *shiva*, which generally commences immediately after burial, to come into effect on Shabbat, when burials are not held. Yet there is the possibility of such a situation, such as if one hears about the death of a close relative some time after the burial.

Shemua rehoka, a "far-away" tiding, refers to hearing about the death of a relative more than thirty days after the burial. In the case of relatives other than a parent, formal mourning is observed for only a symbolic brief period that includes, for example, *keriyah* and sitting low, but not communal expression such as the mourner's meal served by others. On the other hand, if one hears about the death within the thirty-day period—what is referred to as a *shemua kerova,* a "near" tiding—the full *shiva* period is observed even if the week of *shiva* extends past the thirty-day limit. In general, if one receives a *shemua kerova* on Shabbat, *shiva* begins immediately with the observance of the private *devarim she-be-tzina* and public mourning continues Saturday night and ends the following Friday.

But suppose that the Shabbat on which one receives the news is the last day of the *shemua kerova* period. One begins to observe *devarim she-be-tzina* on Shabbat, but full public mourning does not begin on Saturday night. Since "full mourning" could not begin within the *shemua kerova* period, only the symbolic mourning of a *shemua rehoka* is observed after Shabbat.

The resolution of this ostensible contradiction lies in understanding that private mourning has integrity only in the context of its communal expression. Concomitant with privacy comes the danger of denial and retreat, attitudes that contradict the halakhic approach to mourning. In the first Shabbat case, one begins public mourning Saturday night within the *shemua kerova* period, and that retroactively establishes the integrity of the previous private mourning and the seven-day period ends on Friday. But in the second Shabbat case, there is no such opportunity, and the private mourning does not rise to a significant enough level to be part of *shiva*.

Impact of community involvement and awareness in this respect is seen in another related ruling. *Shiva* is inconsistent with holiday celebration, since the communal requirement of holiday joy overwhelms the individuals' requirement to mourn in their hearts. If one begins *shiva* before the holiday, the mourning is cancelled with the commencement of the festival. But if one has not begun *shiva* before the holiday (as, for example, if burial took place during *hol hamoed*), *shiva* is not cancelled but rather deferred until after the holiday. What, then, if one hears a *shemua kerova* on a Shabbat that immediately precedes a holiday? Inasmuch as public mourning is impossible Saturday night, does the observance of private mourning establish that *shiva* had begun before the holiday?

Halakhah rules that the holiday cancels the *shiva* that had begun on Shabbat, something that seems contradictory to the situation when Saturday night brings us to the *shemua rehoka* period. Yet the two are not analogous in an important respect. In the *shemua rehoka* case, it is distance from the event that makes public observance impossible; the impact of death on the community must have some closure. But in the holiday case, it is *involvement* with the community that precludes public mourning, and that community involvement gives integrity to the private mourning expressed on Shabbat.

Honor Your Father and Mother

Mourning Adoptive and Stepparents

The new family structures that have arisen within the general community have also made their way to the Jewish community. While the traditional nuclear family made up of mother, father, and their biological children remains the halakhic paradigm, the fact is that "blended" and adoptive families are becoming more and more common. The interpersonal relationships within these families are usually negotiated in a nonhalakhic context, and the "nontraditional" nature of the family is lost to varying degrees in the course of day-to-day activities. However, the halakhic obligations imposed on biological children might not apply equally to adoptive or stepchildren. In the case of a death, this factor has within it the possibility of adding to the emotional pressures on the bereaved.

The basic obligation to honor and fear one's biological parents, the first of the "interpersonal" commandments of the Decalogue, is an expression of gratitude, *hakarat ha-tov*, for having been created. People owe their physical existence to their biological parents, and the ethics of gratitude demand that this debt be acknowledged in a particular recognizable form. And just as the Rabbis[73] noted that three entities—God, mother, and father—are involved in the creation of any child, so too they insisted that when one honors his or her parents, the person is considered as having honored God Himself.

> When man recognizes his creatureliness before his parents, he recognizes the ultimate creatureliness, and the ultimate creator, as well. For by acknowledging his parents, man admits that he is not the source of his own being, that he owes existence itself to forces beyond his own personal reality. This can remain a most abstract, intellectual perception, to be sure; it is difficult to jar the certain sensation of self-sufficiency. But the religious consciousness demands an awareness of a greater source of reality beyond. The issue of origins, then, is paradigmatic of the choice between radical self-centeredness and acknowledgment of the Other.[74]

Filial responsibility, then, relates to acknowledging one's having been created by others. It is the act of creation—in this case, birth—and nothing else that triggers this obligation. It is for this reason that we owe such filial responsibility to our biological parents, both during their lives and after their deaths, irrespective of our personal psychological relationship with them and, indeed, irrespective of whether the children and parents have ever met.

---

73. Kiddushin 30b.

74. Gerald Blidstein, *Honor Thy Father and Mother* (New York: Ktav, 1975), p. 5.

The same cannot be said about adoptive or stepparents. Indeed, the very notion of stepparent can bespeak very different realities. A stepparent might be the person who married the children's biological parent and raised them for most of their lives; it might also be the person who married their aged parent while a fellow resident of an old-age home. One has an obligation to respect each of these people while they remain married to one's natural parent, but this stems from a legalistic sense of the obligation to respect the latter and is not expressive of any relationship to the stepparents themselves.

> One is obligated to respect his father's wife even if she is not his mother as long as his father is alive, as this is part of the obligation to respect his father. And similarly one is required to respect his mother's husband as long as she is alive. But this obligation ends with her death.[75]

Shulhan Arukh here adds, "In any event, the proper thing is to respect them even after the death of the natural parent." This advice is easily and properly extended to adoptive parents when neither one is the biological parent. Indeed, what possible objection could anyone raise to people showing respect for their adoptive or stepparents by, for example, not sitting in their seat or or addressing them by their first name? Undertaking these formal expressions of reverence cannot possibly violate any halakhic norm and

---

75. *Mishneh Torah, Hilkhot Mamrim* 6:15; *Shulhan Arukh, Yoreh De'ah* 240:21.

are, as *Shulhan Arukh* states, the proper thing to do. Significantly, though, when *Sefer ha-Hinukh* discusses this mitzvah, he extends the rationale beyond the issue of creation:

> One should realize that his mother and father are the cause of his being in the world; therefore it is truly proper that he render them all the honor and do them all the service he can, for they brought him into the world, *and they labored greatly on his behalf during his childhood.*[76]

There is a dual quality to parenthood, then, one that is exhausted by the creative act of birth and the other that is triggered by something that happens in the way parents raise their children. The Halakhah identifies this latter phenomenon in teaching Torah to one's children, in educating them in what is meaningful in life and toward what ends they should direct their activities. "Paternity in human society, then, includes the separate persons of both father and teacher, much as human maturity implies both physical and spiritual growth. Therefore, Jewish tradition sees the flowering of paternity in the master from whom one acquires Torah."[77]

When these two personalities are not embodied in the same person, when the biological parent is not the one who raised the child, the teacher takes precedence, as "one's parent brought him into this world, while it is one's teacher

---

76. *Sefer ha-Hinukh*, *Mitzvah* 33, italics added.
77. Blidstein, *Honor Thy Father and Mother*, p. 139.

who taught him wisdom who brings him to the future world."[78] Significantly, however, the parent takes precedence over the teacher if it was the former who hired the teacher, since it was this action that led the child to the future world.[79]

Here, then, is the halakhic paradigm for the adoptive or stepparent who raises a child: the teacher who gives the child the world to come. Rabbi Joseph B. Soloveitchik writes:

> When the letter *hei* was added to Abram's name, he became Abraham, the father of many nations, the spiritual father of all he taught. Natural procreative Abramic parenthood was denied to the childless couple, yet the creative Abrahamic parenthood is a challenge which everyone is summoned to meet. . . .
>
> The new form of parenthood does not conflict with the biological relation. It manifests itself in a new dimension which may be separated from the natural one. In order to become Abraham, one does not necessarily have to live through the stage of Abram. The irrevocable in human existence is not the natural but the spiritual child; the threefold community is based upon existential, not biological, unity. The existence of I and thou can be inseparably bound with a third existence even though the latter is, biologically speaking, a stranger to them.[80]

---

78. Mishnah at Bava Metsia 33a; *Tur* and *Shulhan Arukh, Yoreh De'ah* 242.

79. Gloss of Rema (R. Moshe Isserles) to *Shulhan Arukh, Yoreh De'ah* 242:34.

80. R. Joseph B. Soloveitchik, "Marriage," in *Family Redeemed*, pp. 60f.

The relationship that the adoptive or stepparents have with the children they have actually raised has a functional expression among many halakhists:[81] The children may be identified when called to the Torah and in formal documents as the son or daughter of those who raised them, and the normal restrictions of *yihud* (which generally allows unsupervised and close contact with only biological parents, siblings, and children) is not applicable to adoptive families, whose members interact as a biological family would. This is far more than transporting halakhic forms (like not addressing one's adoptive parents by their first names) to the adoptive family. It is an expression of a new halakhic reality, so to speak.

Nonetheless, it is not obvious that all the halakhic paradigms of filial responsibility carry over into mourning practices. Of course, there can be no halakhic objection to either feeling intense grief at the death of any individual or expressing it openly, whether or not the individuals have a biological relationship. Certainly adopted children or stepchildren can avoid public celebrations for a year—part of the requirements of *kibbud av va-em* demanded of biological children—and can memorialize their parents at each *yahrzeit*. Yet there is a general reluctance among halakhists to carry over traditional ritual forms into unassigned areas. For example, setting candles for an evening dinner may add

---

81. For a discussion of these issues, see, for example, Mordecai Hakohen, "*Imutz Yeladim lefi ha-Halakha* [Adopting Children According to Halakha]," in Y. L. Hakohen Maimon, ed., *Torah Shebe-al Peh*, vol. 3, 5721 [1951].

to the mood of the meal but does not have the same mitzvah fulfillment (*kiyyum ha-mitzvah* in technical language) as does lighting Shabbat candles for the Friday night meal. Appropriating (or misappropriating) these "copyrighted forms," so to speak, is often considered infringement on the Rabbis' intellectual property rights.

With regard to formal halakhic mourning when it is not obligatory, there are additional considerations. *Avelut* generates certain halakhic consequences, as mourning requires putting aside various mitzvot. For example, the *onen* is exempt from prayer and the *avel* may not study Torah. Moreover, the public nature of mourning may generate misrepresentation of the facts. If children mourn their adoptive father, it might be assumed that the father did not die childless and his widow does not need *halitza* before remarrying. This later concern is less relevant if the adoption is an open one, as Rabbi Soloveitchik advised, and the parents do not hide the truth from their child.

Rabbi Soloveitchik insisted that there is a *kiyyum* of the mitzvah of *avelut* even when there is no halakhic obligation to mourn the specific individual. He drew this conclusion from the ruling that "Where there is a case of a deceased who has left no mourners to be comforted, ten worthy men should assemble at his place all seven days of the mourning period and the rest of the people should gather about them [to comfort them]. And if the ten cannot stay on a regular basis, others from the community may replace them."[82] It

---

82. *Shulhan Arukh, Yoreh De'ah* 476:3. Cf. *Mishneh Torah, Hilkhot Avelut* 13:4.

was for this reason that he regularly advised children to mourn the adopted parents who had raised them. If there was no *hiyyuv* [obligation] *ha-mitzvah*, there was nonetheless a *kiyyum ha-mitzvah*.[83]

Additionally, some forms of mourning become obligatory because the adoptive parents were their children's Torah teacher, either by actually teaching them Torah or by orienting them toward an ethical life (which includes Jewish and halakhic identity), or simply by paying others to educate them. For example, one is obligated to do *keriyah* for one's master teacher; this includes the person who brought one to be converted, thereby granting him or her a portion in the world to come.[84] One reason mourners are exempt from positive mitzvot during the period of *aninut* (is that they are preoccupied with the burial arrangements, something that applies to adoptive children and stepchildren. However, they do not have the special exemption from putting on *tefillin* on the first day of mourning even after *aninut* ends with burial. Thus Rabbi Shlomo Zalman

---

83. R. Elyakim Kenigsberg, *Sheurei HaRav [R. Yosef Dov HaLevi Soloveitchik] al Inyanei Avelut ve-Tisha Be-Av* [Lectures of Rabbi Joseph B. Soloveitchik on Matters Pertaining to Mourning and Tisha Be-Av] (Jerusalem: Mesorah, 1999), p. 38. Cf. R. Zvi Schacter and R. Menachem Genack, eds., "*Mipi Hashemua miMaran HaGrid Soloveitchik* [Lectures Heard from Rabbi Joseph B. Soloveitchik]," *Mesorah,* no. 5, Adar 5751 [1991], p. 41.

84. R. Hayyim Binyamin Goldberg, *Penei Barukh* (Jerusalem: 5746 [1986]), p. 102, n. 7, quoting *Sha'ar Ephraim, Yoreh De'ah* no. 71.

Auerbach rules that after the funeral, the adopted child who is mourning should put on *tefillin* privately.[85]

There is no objection to the adopted child's saying *Kaddish* for his or her adopted parent, since one can say *Kaddish* for any person whose memory one wishes to honor. The only problem that can arise is in those synagogues that maintain the old custom of allowing only one person to say *Kaddish*. There, one who is not obligated to say *Kaddish* cannot claim the right from one who is obligated. This issue is not relevant in our synagogues, where all who wish to say *Kaddish* do so together. Questions of which mourner should act as *hazzan* can usually be resolved with good will.

Two other considerations come into play. During *shiva* the mourner is forbidden to learn Torah or to engage in marital relations, because this is part of the halakhic private mourning that is required even on Shabbat, when public mourning is prohibited. (The child's obligation to learn Torah is suspended when others come to comfort the mourner, says Rabbi Shlomo Zalman Auerbach, because the obligation to honor the dead and those who raised him

---

85. Quoted in Abraham Sofer Abraham, *Nishmat Avraham* (Jerusalem: Rimonim, 1987), vol. 5, p. 141. R. Moshe Sternbach, *Teshuvot veHanagot* 3:474, agrees that in general the adopted child should sit *shiva* but put on *tefillin* the first day, but he adds (noting R. Avraham Avli ben Hayim HaLevi Gombiner, Magen Avraham, no. 17, to *Shulhan Arukh, Orah Hayyim* 548 regarding wearing *tefillin* on Hol ha-Moed) that "if he is truly mourning there is room to exempt him from *tefillin*."

takes precedence.[86]) One's obligation to learn Torah is, of course, fulfilled by studying those areas permitted any mourner.

These small differences between mourning biological parents, on the one hand, and stepparents or adoptive parents, on the other, are private and known only to the mourner. They reflect an inner awareness that their parent-child relationship was Abrahamic rather than Abramic, one based on responsibilities willingly assumed rather than imposed as a consequence of a biological act. As an expression of *hakkarat ha-tov*, the child's mourning is dutiful testimony that the deceased had met the challenges of Abrahamic parenthood.

Mourning Abusive Parents

The obverse of mourning loving adoptive or stepparents is mourning abusive parents. The former involves honoring someone for whom one has great affection despite possible technical arguments that there is no obligation to mourn. The latter involves feelings of repugnance and contempt incompatible with the *kibbud ha-met* expressed in normal mourning regimens to which the victim seems obligated.

Maimonides[87] lists three categories of evil people who are not to be mourned after their death. The first is that of those executed by the Court in the time of the Sanhedrin;

---

86. Nishmat Avraham, op cit.
87. *Mishneh Torah, Hilkhot Avel* I:9–11.

the second is that of *"Ha-porshim mi-darkhei tzibur,* those who deviated from the practices of the community" (a category to which we shall return shortly); and the third is that of those who have committed suicide. Despite the fact that all of these are not to be mourned, there are differences between the groups. The first are not mourned publicly, but the relatives are to grieve in their hearts. In the case of the second, "their siblings and relatives are to put on white garments, wrap themselves in white garments, eat drink and rejoice, because the enemies of the Lord have perished. Concerning them Scripture says, 'Do not I hate them, O Lord, who hate You?' (Psalms 139:21)." Love of God is to trump love of relatives.

With regard to suicides, funeral rites are not performed, and the deceased is neither mourned nor eulogized. Yet the relatives stand in line to be formally comforted, *Birkat Avelim* is said for them, and "all that is intended as an honor for the living is done." Suicide must be deliberate and unpressured from within to merit not being mourned. When an individual is driven to suicide, or there is doubt as to whether death was actually due to suicide, the deceased is mourned in the customary manner. As a practical matter, we use any legitimate argument that we can—his having great fear or pain, or his being mentally unbalanced—to declare the death not a suicide.

Maimonides defines *"Ha-porshim mi-darkhei tzibur,* those who deviated from the practices of the community" as those who cast off the yoke of the commandments and do not join their fellow Jews in performing mitzvot, observing the holidays, attending synagogues and the houses of study, and who do as they please as the other nations do; he includes as well heretics, apostates, and informers. *Shulhan Arukh*[88] adds that we do mourn those who occasionally sin *le-tei'avon* (that is, satisfying one's personal desires) but not those who sin *le-hakh'is* (that is, making a principled statement of defiance of God's authority). Rema's gloss there quotes Mordecai that one who *regularly* sins is not mourned. *Shevet Yehuda* explains that Mordecai feels that as a general principle doing something wrong *le-tei'avon* regularly moves it into the category of *le-hakh'is*; nevertheless, each case must be evaluated on its own merits.

As a practical matter, nowadays even people who regularly desecrate the Sabbath publicly are mourned. The halakhic logic is that given the poor state of Jewish knowledge and observance across the spectrum of the Jewish community, one simply cannot read principled statements of rejection of the community into even consistent nonhalakhic behavior. The average person may even concede the inappropriateness of a particular action without dreaming that he or she had crossed the line into being enemies of God. Short of converting to another religion, they remain part of the Jewish community, meriting being mourned despite their deficiencies.

In this light, evaluating the status of an abusive parent becomes at times difficult. The parameters of "abuse" are rather wide, ranging from, say, harsh and insensitive words

---

88. *Shulhan Arukh, Yoreh De'ah* 340:5.

to cruel and repeated vicious sexual assaults. One need not justify in the least ruthless and hurtful abusive language to say that a misguided parent could mistakenly think it to be within communal norms, distorting "Spare the rod and spoil the child." On the other hand, there are abusive actions (for example, repeated rape) that are so outrageous that no reasonable person could possibly think they fall within acceptable behavior. Clearly some actions could be done only by those beyond the pale.

However, if the transgression was done privately with few if any knowing, it is not obvious that the abuser is to be recognized as a *poersh mi-darkhei tzibur*, even though he or she might clearly be an evil person. It is the *community*, above all, which does not deal with those who "deviated from the practices of the community," returning public rejection with public rejection. While every *poresh mi-darkhei tzibur* might be considered evil, it may not be the case that every wicked person is considered to be *poresh mi-darkhei tzibur* if the wickedness is not well known or not done to publicly reject the community and its values. It may be that the action must not be simply outrageous but rather done deliberately to outrage the community. Perhaps, just as we look for a way to rule that those who took their own lives not be categorized as suicides, we must seriously consider whether the abuser was of sound mind while sinning and whether he or she had since repented.

However, as important as it is to focus on the technical status of the abuser, it is crucial to consider the mind of the mourner. After all, to mourn means more than going through some ritualistic motions. It is the mindset that is crucial. As Rabbi Soloveitchik notes:

> In effect, the Torah has required that inward soulful mourning be expressed through observance of the eleven prohibitions, but the central *kiyyum* consists of a psychological state of dejection and sadness. Could one imagine that the obligation to mourn had been fulfilled by a mourner who, though adhering diligently to all the prescribed practices and violating none of the eleven prohibitions, at the same time brought into his home and enjoyed, during the mourning period, all manner of pleasant diversions?[89]

Is the victim *unable* or *unwilling* to generate a psychological state of dejection and sadness for the abuser? Is he or she truly convinced that the abuser was evil rather than sick, or are we dealing with an act of revenge and hatred? After all, "The Halakhah holds the view that man's mastery of his emotional life is unqualified and that he is capable of changing thought patterns, emotional structures, and experiential motifs within an infinitesimal period of time."[90] In general, halakhah often requires people to put aside natural inclinations and, for example, to not hate their enemies.

It is interesting to note the response of Rabbi Yitzhak Zilberstein[91] to a related question concerning a woman un-

89. R. Joseph B. Soloveitchik, "The Essential Nature of Mourning," in *Out of the Whirlwind*, pp. 69f.

90. R. Joseph B. Soloveitchik, "*Aninut* and *Avelut*," in *Out of the Whirlwind*, p. 3.

91. R. Yitzhak Zilberstein, "*Pegi'ah be-Kevod Horim le-Tzorekh Hatsalah ve-Refu'a*," *Kol Ha-Torah*, Nisan 5763 [2003], p. 173.

dergoing psychotherapy to deal with the trauma of having been abused as a child. Such therapy requires speaking of the parent in a disrespectful way while working through the effects of the psychological trauma inflicted in childhood. While there is some dispute on the obligation to honor wicked parents, there is general consensus that one may not humiliate his or her parent. Talking this way about a parent, says Rabbi Zilberstein, would generally be prohibited even if he or she was indeed wicked. However, he continues:

> The Torah's prohibition to humiliate and disrespect one's father is only when the aim is for the sake of humiliation, but not when it is done for therapeutic purposes, and for the benefit of the daughter, which in the end is for his benefit also, so that he will have a healthy daughter. . . . And the proof that it is permitted to shame and distress the father for desirable benefits is derived from King Hezekiah, who dragged his [wicked] father's bones on a bed of sackcloth (as explained at Pesahim 56). Rashi explained there that he dragged his father's bones for expiation of his sins . . . that he be censured for his wickedness and his wicked deeds be removed. . . . Therefore, it is permitted to humiliate a father for a benefit, and especially when the father destroyed his daughter's world, he is obligated to suffer in order that she be cured.

Rabbi Zilberstein allows the psychotherapy even if the father had repented, because a true penitent would want his daughter to be psychologically healthy, even if her being so required his humiliation. He concludes:

And after the daughter is cured and her wounds are healed, it is proper to urge her to return to respect her father for she is obligated to him for bringing her into the world. In spite of the damage he inflicted on her, her debt to her father has not expired.

Those who are so bruised by their experience that they simply cannot bring themselves to mourn are exempt by virtue of their own medical/ psychological limitations. Moreover, we can assume that the abuser, even if he or she repented, would want the victim to heal even if doing so necessitated the public humiliation of not being mourned. Victims surely have no obligation to endanger their emotional well-being by mourning.

The victim may be unable or unwilling to acknowledge that abusive relationships are rarely, if ever, purely evil or abusive. Indeed, it is often the tension between good feelings and violent, vicious actions that characterizes these relationships. It would seem that once the abuser is gone, one might indeed mourn the loss of that which was good in the person. In this context, it is interesting to note that R. Gershon had mourned his son who had converted even though such a person is surely not to be mourned. Mordecai[92] comments that he mourned the fact that his son had not repented. Here too there is much for the victim to mourn, including final closure on the possibility of a normal and loving relationship. Moreover, every death—especially the death of someone to whom we are genetically related—

---

92. Moed Katan, chap. 3, no. 886.

reminds us of our own human mortality, something that surely evokes a psychological state of sadness.

Rabbi Zilberstein's comment on the obligation of the healed victim also has resonance here. Parents do not have to earn their children's respect; it is their right simply by virtue of being biological parents. Respect for parents is, in many ways, an exercise in learning to see past imperfections in others and recognize the best in them. Few parents ever come close to doing evil things, but all fail at one time or another, and their children, who have continuous access to them when they are not necessarily on their best behavior, are poised to notice it.

> When a child first catches adults out—when it first walks into his grave little head that adults do not always have divine intelligence, that their judgments are not always wise, their thinking true, their sentences just—his world falls into panic desolation. The gods are fallen and all safety gone. And there is one sure thing about the fall of gods: they do not fall a little; they crash and shatter or sink deeply into green muck. It is a tedious job to build them up again; they never quite shine. And the child's world is never quite whole again. It is an aching kind of growing.[93]

Insistence on honoring parents prepares children for this confrontation with reality. Tellingly, with regard to *porshim mi-darkhei tzibur*, it is "their *siblings* and relatives [who] are to put on white garments, wrap themselves in white

---

93. John Steinbeck, *East of Eden* (N.Y.: Penguin Books, 1980), p. 20.

garments, eat drink and rejoice, because the enemies of the Lord have perished." By addition of the word "siblings," children may be excluded.

Kibbud horim is tied to our obligation to honor God. In honoring our parents, we acknowledge our debt to give thanks for our creation; and as we know, God joins with mother and father in creating a child. Indeed, one might well argue that the whole concept of *kibbud horim* is based on the demand that we learn to look past inevitable human foibles and see the divine that stands behind all parents.

> When one honors or reveres his natural parent, father or mother, he, *ipso facto*, honors or reveres God. . . . What is transient fatherhood and motherhood if not a reflected beam of light coming to us from beyond the frontiers of the cosmos, and what is paternal or maternal concern if not an echo of the great concern of the Almighty?
>
> Whenever Rav Yosef heard the footsteps of his mother, he would say: Let me rise because the *Shekhinah* is coming (Kiddushin 31b). Behind every mother, young or old, happy or sad, trails the *Shekhinah*. And behind every father, erect or stooped, in playful or stern mood, walks *Malka Kadisha,* the Holy King. This is not mysticism. It is Halakhah. The awareness of the *Shekhinah* results in the obligation to rise before father and mother.[94]

Thus we honor our parents for their being parents, and not for how well or how poorly they lived up to the require-

---

94. R. Joseph B. Soloveitchik, "Torah and *Shekhinah*," in *Family Redeemed*, p. 168.

ments of that role. Shunning a public response of anger or observing mourning practices and reciting *Kaddish* after an abusive parent affirms the importance of parenthood itself, even while quietly rejecting his or her particular parent as a model for how that role should be fulfilled.

There is, however, another reason to consider mourning, one that also applies to relatives who are not parents and who would not fall under the rubric of the requirement of *kibbud horim*. It might be simply healthy for the person to let go of the anger and resentment—no matter how justified—well past the individual's death. Mourning, we saw, involves turning the individual back from resentment that an encounter with death triggers (which is expressed in *aninut*) to "start picking up the debris of his own shattered personality" (which is expressed in *avelut*). This process would apply even more to an individual whose life has already been fundamentally shattered by betrayal. Opting out of the mourning process would only cement the lifelong feeling of betrayal. Indeed, if victims knew that they were obligated when the time came to mourn a relative, no matter what the relationship, no matter how abusive, that knowledge might just inspire individuals to seek help in coming to peace with their past.

In addition, forgoing mourning deprives the victim of the healing balm of the comforting community and "all that is intended as an honor for the living." Nonetheless, even the victim who mourns the deceased abuser has a quiet opportunity to express the feeling that the abuser has not "earned it." For example, one need not exercise the exemption from prayer in effect during the *aninut* period, no false eulogies need be presented, and a quieter, understated *shiva* experience requested. Generally, saying *Kaddish* is halted during the final month because only a *rasha*, an evil person, needs the redeeming quality of *Kaddish* for a full year. In this case, saying *Kaddish* for the full period gives subtle acknowledgment of the wickedness of the deceased.

National and Individual Mourning

Tisha BeAv

In his classic *sheur* on *Avelut Hadasha and Avelut Yeshana,*[95] Rabbi. Soloveitchik addresses the question of the nature of mourning on Tisha BeAv, the ninth day of the month of Av, the anniversary of the destruction of the Temples in Jerusalem. In his presentation, herein summarized, the communal mourning of Tisha BeAv and the period leading up to it does not represent simply a statement of the grief associated with the destruction of the Temples, but, by its contrast with the mourning following the death of a close relative, explicates the contours of individual mourning.

Both the communal and individual mourning periods are divided into distinct time periods, but their internal progressions are reversed. Halakhah divides an individual's mourning into the following stages: First, the period of

---

95. R. Joseph B. Soloveitchik, "Individual and Historical Mourning," in *Out of the Whirlwind,* pp. 9–30.

aninut, extending from the time of death until the time of burial. Then, beginning with burial, there is *avelut shivah*, the seven-day mourning period that extends into *sheloshim*, the thirty-day mourning period required for all relatives. Finally, for one's parents there is *yod-bet hodesh*, the twelve-month period of mourning. The intensity of the mourning abates as one is distanced from the trauma of the confrontation with death. On the other hand, communal mourning increases in intensity, starting with "the Three Weeks" (which begin three weeks before Tisha BeAv on the seventeenth of the month of Tamuz, the anniversary of the breaching of Jerusalem's walls), proceeding through *Rosh Hodesh Av* (the first day of the month of Av) and on to *Shavua She-hal-bo* (the week in which Tisha BeAv falls), and finally the fast day of Tisha BeAv itself.

This difference expresses the very different dynamics of individual and communal grief: the former arises spontaneously and the latter is artificially constructed. *Avelut hadashah* ("new mourning") is *avelut de-yahid* (an "individual's mourning") which is caused by a death or disaster that strikes a family or an individual. It is an instinctual response of man to evil, to the shock of a confrontation with death. On the other hand, *avelut yeshanah* ("old mourning") is *avelut de-rabbim*, an artificially created communal mourning. Here there is no spontaneous reaction to some new event which has just happened. Indeed, nothing new has happened that should justify grief. The mourning is a result of recollection of past, almost forgotten events.

The halakhot of *avelut de-yahid* represent Judaism's insistence that the reality of evil be recognized. An encounter with death must bring about a showing of protest and a bitter complaint. The mourners tear their clothes in anger and stop observing mitzvot because their whole personality is enveloped by the darkness of death. Indeed, they are relieved of their obligation in mitzvot because they are simply incapable of performing them. Of course, emotions recede. The Torah has therefore recommended that man not only submit himself to the emotional onslaught, but gradually and slowly remove himself from its impact.

Avelut yeshanah, on the other hand, reflects a position that emotions can be *evoked.* It is possible to recall events from our collective memory and reexperience them as present. However, the process is generally slow, reawakening the idea that past memory takes time. Halakhah, therefore, could not decree observance of mourning the Temple at once. The time between the seventeenth of Tammuz and Rosh Hodesh Av is devoted to remembrance with little halakhic detail. Only on Rosh Hodesh Av does the *avelut she-ba-lev* (mourning in one's heart) take form. The Mishnah states in general terms that "when Av begins we lessen our happiness."[96] The Baraita says, "From the first day of the month until the fast day, *ha-am me-ma'atim,* the general populace limits its activities in trade, building, and planting, *eirusin* (formal marriage engagements), as well as mar-

---

96. Taanit 1:7.

riages. During the week in which the ninth of Av occurs, it is prohibited to cut one's hair and wash one's clothes."[97]

Thus, the period of mourning for the Temple which parallels that of the twelve-month mourning for parents begins on the first day of the month of Av. Both share the avoidance of participation in any festive events, receptions, and so forth. *Shavu'a she-hal bo* (the week in which Tisha BeAv falls, the restrictions of which are often extended from the first day of Av) corresponds to *sheloshim*, since both include the prohibitions of taking a haircut or wearing freshly pressed clothes. The mourning of Tisha BeAv itself is like that of *shiva*. The Baraita says that "all the prohibitions which are in effect during *shiva* are observed on Tisha BeAv."[98]

But *Tisha BeAv* exists not only in the past. We say in the *Kinnot* (the liturgy for Tisha BeAv), "On this night my Temple was destroyed." That night nineteen hundred years ago is as much a reality as this fleeting moment in the present. Jews know not only how to recall the past but to relive it as well.

Despite the established parallelism, there are important distinctions. For example, washing one's clothes and engaging in commerce are prohibited in *shavua she-hal bo* and permitted during *sheloshim*. On the other hand, *eirusin* is permissible during *shavua she-hal bo* and forbidden, according to Ri and Ramban, during *sheloshim*. *Tefillin* are not

97. Yevamot 43b.
98. Taanit 29b.

worn on the first day of *avelut* but they are worn on Tisha BeAv (albeit in the afternoon). These differences are due to the different types of mourning being expressed.

The mourning of *shavua she-hal bo* revolves around the concept of *heseah ha-da'at*, being distracted from the mourning experience. This mourning is intellectual, and invoking emotions from it requires a concentrated effort. Engaging in commerce is a steady occupation. In olden times, washing clothes meant continuous public work at the river. *Avelut yeshanah* is stricter with those matters that are public and continuous.

On the other hand, *heseah ha-da'at* plays no role in individual grief, because the mourner's emotions are spontaneous. The prohibitions pertaining to private mourning are concerned not with the possibility of *heseah ha-da'at* but with different aspects such as *nivvul* and *tza'ar* (looking disheveled and in sorrow). The prohibition of *eirusin* (an act which requires only two witnesses and is therefore not considered public) is not rooted in *heseah ha-da'at*, which applies to such public actions as washing one's clothes and engaging in commerce. The individual mourner is enjoined from *eirusin* because a confrontation with death causes one to lose confidence in the meaningfulness of life. Building a family is not the concern of that moment.

The difference in the halakhah on wearing *tefillin* on Tisha BeAv and the first day of *shiva* likewise reflects the different dynamics of mourning. The prohibition against putting on *tefillin* as a mourner is not part of required mourning activities. Rather, the mourner's personal status (to use a technical phrase, his *gavra*) is that of an *avel;* as such, he cannot be crowned with *tefillin* or adorn himself with them. On the other hand, *avelut yeshanah,* while it imposes mourning observances, cannot change the *gavra* into an *avel.* Therefore *tefillin* are worn on Tisha BeAv.

But *eirusin* is permitted on Tisha BeAv, because the notion of despair and resignation is contrary to the very gist of *avelut de-rabbim.* There, the mourner is not the individual but the nation as a whole. No matter how difficult times are, the messianic hope is always there; therefore the nation will not despair.

It is this belief that offers consolation to the community, yet individuals who suffer a loss find consolation in the present and not in the future. It is the physical community of friends and relatives that supports the mourners and gives them the strength to recapture their faith. The process is a slow one and it often moves haltingly; but it is they who bring the mourners back to their world, strong in spirit and confident in confronting all that might come their way.

Yom HaShoah

Despite the fact that the mourning on Tisha BeAv is not only for the destruction of the Temples but for the entire span of Jewish tragedies, there has been a movement to establish a different day to commemorate the tragedy of the European destruction of six million Jews during the Second World War. The Israeli Chief Rabbinate did establish the tenth of Tevet as a *Yom HaKaddish HaKelali* to commemorate those who died on unknown dates during the Holocaust. This was a separate date of observance without the creation of a new day of commemoration on the Jewish calendar.

It has been argued that the Jewish community—including Religious Zionists who recognize the authority of the Chief Rabbinate—"voted with its feet" against this arrangement by ignoring it for the most part.[99] But this day was not really set up as a Holocaust memorial day, since it was never meant to be a permanent day of national observance. Individuals who went through the Holocaust needed a *yahrzeit* date to commemorate the death of relatives killed on unknown dates. The rabbinate responded to this personal need with a *Yom HaKaddish*, a designation that would "self-destruct" when the last survivor died and no specific day for personal *yahrzeit* would be needed. Tisha BeAv, the day for national rather than personal observance, would have been inappropriate for such an individual's *Yom HaKaddish*. No other day had claim for such a designation, so a day that already had communal attention was chosen. Thus the Chief Rabbinate at the time was actually maintaining silence on the national issue while meeting the needs of the individuals affected. The *Yom HaKaddish HaKelali* was not really ignored by the Jewish people, since it was never directed to the nation as a whole.

---

99. Irving (Yitz) Greenberg, *Yom HaShoa* (National Jewish Research Center, 1982).

There is, of course, another day of national mourning: Yom HaShoah, Holocaust Memorial Day, observed on 27 Nisan, a week after Passover. Yom HaShoah observances are taken so much for granted by a wide spectrum of Jewry that it surprises many that a significant part of the Torah community—those of the "right wing" who are associated with Agudah and Hasidic circles—stand apart from these activities.[100]

Various explanations have been given for this opposition but, as we shall see, they are for the most part unconvincing. Some suggest that the opposition to Yom HaShoah is based on the technical character of the suggested observances or its falling in the month of Nisan. *Hesped* (formal eulogy) is forbidden during the month of Nisan, as it is on Yom Tov and *Hol HaMoed*. Yet *Yizkor* (together with the *Malei Rahamim* prayer) is permitted on the holidays because it is only a memorial service and not the *hesped* which is said within a year of death.[101] Such logic should certainly carry over to Yom HaShoah. Moreover, *Shulhan Arukh* lists 26 Nisan among the "days on which one fasts."[102]

Yom HaShoah carries with it no specific obligatory fast, ritual, or eulogy. In Israel, the theaters are closed—surely

---

100. Viz, Jacob J. Schacter, "Holocaust Commemoration and *Tisha be-Av*: The Debate Over '*Yom ha-Sho'a*,'" *Tradition*, 41:2 (Summer 2008), pp. 164–197.

101. *Shulhan Arukh, Orah Hayyim* 547:5, *Mishnah Berurah* n. 8; *Yoreh De'ah* 394.

102. *Shulhan Arukh, Orah Hayyim* 580:2.

there can be no objection to this custom from Torah circles—and people stand silently for a minute when the siren is sounded. It has been noted that this practice does not represent *hukkat ha-goyim,* mimicking non-Jewiish customs; there is no halakhic objection to participating in the moment of silence, even standing and learning in silence during a *bet midrash seder.*[103] Outside Israel, there is even less formal structure. Some groups might create an inappropriate ceremony, but the same could be said about some particular community programs on, say, Purim. Nothing prevents a synagogue or yeshivah from joining the wider Jewish community in focusing on the Holocaust by organizing an observance of Yom HaShoah that is completely in accord with Torah standards and sensitivities.

It has been suggested that the opposition to Yom Ha-Shoah stems from a short letter of R. Avraham I. Karelitz (known as Hazon Ish) prohibiting the establishment of a fast day in commemoration of the European tragedy.[104] Contemporary rabbinic leaders do not have the prerogative to establish an obligatory fast day for all of Israel, he wrote,

---

103. R. Yehudah Herzl Henkin, *Responsa Benai Banim* (Jerusalem, 1981), no. 10, pp. 40ff. See also his *"Kima li-Khavod ha-Nofelim be-Yom ha-Zikkaron* (Standing in Honor of the "Fallen on Memorial Day)" in *Tehumin* 4 (Jerusalem: Zomet, 5743 [1983]), pp. 125–129; and *"Od be-Issur be-Hukkoteihem Lo Teileikhu u-ve-Kimah li-khvod ha-Nofelim be-Yom ha-Zikkaron"* in his *Responsa and Letters in Halakhic Matters, Second Series* (mimeographed), no. 22 (63), dated 2 Shevat 5743 (1983).

104. R. Sh. Greineman, ed., *Kovetz Iggerot Hazon Ish* (Jerusalem, 5715 [1957]), part one, letter 97, pp. 113f.

since such authority expired with the end of the prophetic period.[105]

Yet this approach too is problematic as a true root cause of opposition to Yom HaShoah commemorations. Unfortunately, Hazon Ish cited no sources for his ruling. In fact, the tradition does have a well-known precedent for establishing a new fast day. In 1171 there was a blood libel in Blois, France, that resulted in the torture and death of thirty-one Jews, including Torah scholars of note. Rabbeinu Tam, the great Tosafist, decreed that the anniversary of that date should be a fast day for Jews everywhere.[106] Apparently, he felt no compelling need to mark the community's destruction by simply adding a *kina* to the Tisha BeAv liturgy. Centuries later the survivors of Chmielnicki's pogroms saw their suffering as a repetition of that earlier tragedy that had occurred on 20 Sivan and appropriately observed a fast on that date.[107] Magen Avraham noted that it was the custom

---

105. R. Aryeh Leb Shpitz, *"Al Devar Keviat Yom Ta'anit …* (Regarding the Establishment of a Fast Day in Memory of the Victims of the Destruction)," *Ha-Ma'or,* 33:5 (262), May–June 1981 1574 I, pp. 13–17, argued that there is a serious error in the transcription of this letter (or that in fact the Hazon Ish never signed it) and that its position should not be taken as authoritative Halakhah. The authenticity of the letter is, however, generally taken for granted.

106. Ephraim ben Jacob, *A Book of Historical Records,* in Jacob R. Marcus, *The Jew in the Medieval World: A Source Book: 315–1791* (New York: Harper Row, 1965), pp. 127–130.

107. Shabbetai Katz, *Megillat Efah,* quoted in Yosef Hayim Yerushalmi, *Zakhor: Jewish History and Jewish Memory* (Seattle and London: University of Washington Press, 1982), p.50.

"to fast on 20 Sivan throughout the Polish kingdom,"[108] in commemoration of the pogroms of Chmielnicki and his Cossacks (and other tragedies); *selihot* for this fast day can be found in some current *siddurim*.[109] It has been argued[110] that that custom is a model for a special fast day in commemoration of the Holocaust.

In a brief comment, Rabbi Moshe Feinstein takes issue with the suggestion of accepting 20 Sivan as such a precedent.[111] New fast days can be established to commemorate local tragedies, he wrote, not national ones. The pogroms of that period, tragic as they might have been, were in the end local events without government sponsorship. But the Holocaust, he continued, was a government-sponsored program directed against all of *klal Yisrael*; communities were spared only because Hitler did not succeed in conquering the whole world. Such a national tragedy must be commemorated within the context of Tisha BeAv, he concluded, the day set aside for mourning national catastrophes.

Again, no sources were cited, and it is not clear from Rabbi Feinstein's brief comment exactly what is the halakhic significance of the sponsorship of the oppression, what

---

108. R. Yosef Karo, *Shulhan Arukh, Orah Hayyim* 580:2, *Magen Avraham*, n. 5.

109. For example, *Otsar ha-Tefillot*, vol. 2, pp. 130–143.

110. R. Shpitz, p. 15..

111. *Iggerot Moshe, Yoreh De'ah* 4:57(11). On Tisha BeAv as the day set aside for mourning all national catastrophes, see also R. Joseph B. Soloveitchik, *The Lord Is Righteous in All His Ways*, ed. Jacob J. Schacter (Toras HoRav Foundation, 2006), pp 226f.

is the halakhic benchmark at which the sum of many local tragedies becomes a national one, or why the various optional fast dates noted in *Shulhan Arukh*[112] should not serve as counterexamples. Also Rabbi Feinstein's reasoning seems to be different from that of the Hazon Ish, which appears to focus on the authority to impose a national fast day, not the national character of the disaster.

Yet one need not question the authoritative nature of either of these rulings to realize that, in the end, neither applies to Yom HaShoah. Both *poskim* spoke out against any attempt by rabbinic authorities to impose an obligatory fast day in commemoration of the Holocaust. Certainly no claim was ever made that the Knesset established Yom HaShoah as a halakhically obligatory fast day. Indeed, neither authority referred to Yom HaShoah or published anything suggesting a halakhic prohibition from participating in such memorials.

There is, of course, a general reluctance to extend specific focus to the Shoah on a day other than Tisha BeAv. Thus Rabbi Yitzhak Hutner, a late member of Agudath Israel's rabbinical leadership and one of the seminal Torah thinkers of the twentieth century, noted in an article in Agudath Israel's *Jewish Observer* his objection not only to Yom Ha-Shoah but to the use of the very term "Holocaust" to describe the destruction of European Jewry.

Is the term "Shoah" acceptable? The answer is, clearly not!. The word *Shoah* in Hebrew, like "Holocaust" in English,

---

112. *Shulhan Arukh, Orah Hayyim 580.*

implies an isolated catastrophe . . . The *churban* [destruction] of European Jewry is an integral part of our history and we dare not isolate it and deprive it of its monumental significance for us.[113]

In an editorial comment accompanying his article, the *Jewish Observer* noted "that those who originated the term *Sho'a* view the Holocaust as an event totally unrelated to Jewish history and therefore requiring a memorial for itself. In contrast, if the European *churban* is seen correctly in the light of Torah, Tisha BeAv is of course the day for remembering all Jewish suffering."[114] Indeed, Yaakov Feitman, one of Rabbi Hutner's interpreters, stated that the "Torah position" is that 'the healthy corpus of *klal Yisroel* will ulti-

---

113. R. Yitzchok Hutner, "Holocaust," *The Jewish Observer,* XII:8, October 1977 ICheshvan 5738], pp. 3–9. (Generally, Rabbi Hutner's admonition to avoid the term "Holocaust" has not been accepted by his community, if only for practical reasons.)

114. Ibid., p. 9. Of course, *kinot* commemorating the Holocaust are now regularly said on Tisha BeAv, after the rabbinical leadership of Agudath Israel (Rabbis Moshe Feinstein, Mordecai Gifter, Yaakov Kaminetsky, Yaakov Ruderman, and Israel Shapira) and others publicly called for commemorating the Holocaust with such a Tisha BeAv elegy. (*Gillui Da'at:* A Public Statement from the Members of the Rabbinical Council of Agudath Israel of America), dated 7 Tevet 5744 (1984), in Pinhas Hertska, ed., *Kuntrus Divrei Derisha. . . . ,* unnumbered). The Chief Rabbinate of the British Commonwealth, for example, had long ago authorized a *kina* for Tisha BeAv commemorating the victims of the Holocaust, found in Abraham Rosenfeld, *The Authorized* Kinot *for the Ninth of Av, with the Sanction of the Chief Rabbi Israel Brodie* (London: C. Labworth & Co., 1965), pp. 173–175.

mately reject the foreign body of an arbitrarily convened *Yom HaShoah* from its system."[115]

However, this is hardly the definitive halakhic position. Indeed, one of the Torah giants of the postwar era, Rabbi Yehiel Yaakov Weinberg, wrote:

> In my opinion, it is proper to establish a specific day of commemoration and mourning to memorialize the rabbis and martyrs who were slaughtered and burned at *kiddush haShem*. . . . We should do this not only out of respect for these martyrs, but also so that future generations not forget what was lost to our nation.[116]

Indeed, given the halakhic permissibility of a separate Holocaust commemoration that is not an obligatory fast day, the question of establishing such a memorial day turns to some extent on whether the Shoah has some unique standing in Jewish history or whether it is but a current and terrible example of all too frequent tragedies that befell the Jewish people.

R. Hutner himself had argued that the Shoah, in this sense, had special significance:

> The end-result of this period for the Jewish psyche was a significant—indeed, crucial—one. From trust in the gentile world, the Jewish nation was cruelly brought to a repudia-

---

115. Yaakov Feitman, "Rabbi Hutner's 'Holocaust' Seminar," *Jewish Observer*, XII:10, January 1978 IShevat 5738], p. 12.

116. R. Yehiel Yaakov Weinberg, *Responsa Seridei Esh* (Jerusalem: Mossad HaRav Kook, 1977), vol. 2, p. 53, no. 30, n. *.

tion of that trust. In a relatively short historical period, disappointment in the non-Jewish world was deeply imprinted upon the Jewish soul.[117]

This repudiation, he argues, is the necessary first step for reaching *Aharit ha-Yamim*. Maimonides sees this as the necessary prerequisite to the final stage of repentance, R. Hutner concludes, and explains the current *ba'al teshuvah* phenomenon of large numbers of people returning to halakhic observance.[118] For R. Hutner, then, there is weight to the Holocaust that is absent from other Jewish national tragedies; as there is an additional new lesson to be learned from it that affects our national destiny. The Holocaust has become an "orienting event,"[119] one that changes the way we view the world.

For Rabbi Eliezer Berkovits, the Holocaust has special significance for Jews and gentiles in that it marks the end of the "Christian Era." Christianity is no longer the decisive power or influence; Jews, he argued, have a special responsibility as the *am olam* [the eternal nation] to sum up the

———————

117. R. Hutner, "Holocaust," p. 5.

118. Ibid., p. 6.

119. The phrase is Irving Greenberg's. See his "The Third Great Cycle in Jewish History," in *Perspectives* (National Jewish Research Center, 1981). Note also Michael Wyschogrod's critique of Greenberg's position that the Holocaust is a "revelational event" in his "Auschwitz: Beginning of a New Era? Reflections on the Holocaust," *Tradition* 16:5 (Fall 1977), pp. 63–78. We need not make the theological claim that the Holocaust is a "revelational event" to note that functionally it has become an "orienting event."

moral and spiritual bankruptcy of that era. For him, "a straight line leads from the first act of oppression against the Jews and Judaism in the fourth century to the holocaust in the twentieth. . . . This has been a moral and spiritual collapse the likes of which the world has never witnessed before for contemptibility and inhumanity."[120]

> No one can foretell what this new era holds in store for mankind. But we are here at the threshold of the new age. We who were there when the Christian era began; we in whose martyrdom Christianity suffered its worst moral debacle; we in whose blood the Christian era found its end—we are here as this new era begins. And we shall be here when this new era reaches its close—we, the *edim*, God's own witnesses, the *am alam*, the eternal witnesses of history.[121]

This responsibility as God's witnesses in history cannot be fulfilled through the grieving of Tisha BeAv, because then the message would be lost on a day devoted primarily to mourning the Temple's destruction. Such a "witness" would require a separate presentation, its own public declaration. A distinct Yom HaShoah is the logical conclusion of this position. Indeed, it is not insignificant to note that some churches have adopted parallel Yom HaShoah services and that the United States government has adopted a Holocaust Memorial Day that corresponds to Yom HaShoah on

120. R. Eliezer Berkovits, "Judaism in the Post-Christian Era," *Judaism* 15:1 (Winter 1966), p. 77.
121. Ibid., p. 84.

the Jewish calendar. Both of these phenomena would have been unthinkable had a distinct Yom HaShoah not been established. Christians in general have quite naturally not been quick to draw Berkovits's conclusions regarding their religion; but for some of their religious thinkers, their theologies have been "ruptured" to the extent that the Christian mission to the Jews has been called into question.[122] An annual Yom HaShoah keeps uncomfortable questions before the Christian community and forces us to reevaluate our place in Western society.

On the surface, then, there is one objection to observing Yom HaShoah (27 Nisan) that should have been appealing to all segments of the halakhic community. The Jewish calendar is part of *netzah Yisrael* and no part of the Torah world would be quick to hand it over to a secular authority, even a benign one. This Yom HaShoah is a construct of the Knesset, an admittedly secular nonhalakhic body. As such, it should have no standing of note within a Torah society.

It is this very objection which underscores a significant division within the Torah community. For a weighty segment of that world, the State of Israel is not simply a secular state. As the Almighty's gift to us, it and its organs have a standing and claim on all committed Jews. To be sure, this is not to argue that Knesset legislation has the halakhic status of Jewish law (except to the extent that all civil legisla-

---

122. Emil Fackenheim, "Holocaust," in Arthur A. Cohen and Paul Mendes-Flor, eds., *Contemporary Jewish Religious Thought* (New York: Charles Scribner's Sons, 1987), p. 404.

tion in a democratic society might have halakhic consequence). But the State sometimes transcends itself, reaching out to represent *klal Yisrael*. If there is a massacre in Lebanon, we realize that we face a potential desecration of God's name; when Tzahal liberates Jerusalem, we sense a *kiddush shem shamayim*, a sanctification of God's name, and a mark made in the eternal history of world Jewry. Exactly when the State reaches out beyond itself is an unaddressed question; but the reality of the possibility is a basic (if perhaps unstated) assumption for Religious Zionists. In giving form to the legitimate need to create a memorial day for the Holocaust, one might maintain, the State has indeed fulfilled this potential. From this perspective, observing Yom Ha-Shoah on 27 Nisan is more than simply compatible with basic Torah allegiance. On the other hand, if the State of Israel is seen simply as a secular entity, there is certainly nothing compelling about participating in its constructs. All the more so for those who see the State as an anti-Torah phenomenon.

This is not to say that Religious Zionists who commemorate Yom HaShoah are oblivious to a very serious problem in the selection of this particular date. It would be fair to say that the choice of 27 Nisan as Yom HaShoah grew out of a sense of *shelilat ha-gola* (a negative approach to the Jewish experience in exile). Burdened with a why-didn't-they-fight-back neurosis and a disdainful view of a *galut* that left Jews to suffer as victims, some members of the Knesset tried to "redeem" the character of European Jewry by creating a *Yom HaShoah vehaGevurah*, a day commemorating victims and resistance, one that focused on the Warsaw Ghetto uprising as much as (if not more than) it took note of the destruction and which was observed on the anniversary of that revolt.

Religious Jews reject this approach outright. They rightfully feel that European Jewry's character needs no defenders. Faced with unspeakable barbarism, Jews never lost sight of their commitment to live as human beings created in God's image. Faith is a form of heroism, though not necessarily the *gevurah* appreciated by secularists. This unfortunate history of 27 Nisan as Yom HaShoah no doubt accounts for much of the negative attitude maintained toward this day of solemnization.

But this unfortunate secular attitude of *shelilat ha-gola* is certainly not an intrinsic part of the commemoration. There is currently increased focus on the spiritual heroism of the victims of the Nazis and an appreciation of the richness of the European Jewish experience. Perhaps the steadfast resistance of some rabbinical authorities contributed to this awareness; perhaps it simply came naturally from a more balanced stance that comes with the passage of time. The only factor that has remained constant regarding 27 Nisan as Yom HaShoah is its Zionist sponsorship. That, we suggest, is why those who reject Religious Zionism as a Torah perspective cannot accept Yom HaShoah even though its contemporary expression need not be otherwise offensive in the least.

From Shoah *to* Yeshuah

The "Zionist" dimension of Yom HaShoah yields an important sensitivity: Yom HaShoah is observed a week before Yom HaAtzmaut, Israel Independence Day. The realization that we have moved quickly in history from destruction to redemption, from *shoah* to *yeshuah*, cannot be avoided; the calendar forces us to confront the mysterious interrelationship of these two epochal events in Jewish history.

Of course, on a practical level we know that in many ways the State did grow out of the Holocaust. In the aftermath of World War II, tens of thousands of refugees who would otherwise most likely not have joined the *yishuv* came to Palestine to build the State. The Western world, which in general quickly extended recognition to Israel, would most likely not have been as generous had not the image of millions of Jewish corpses rested heavily on its conscience. Indeed, the Holocaust ended the Zionist debate within the Jewish community as just about all Jews embraced the new State with enthusiasm and hope.

This historical nexus is reflected in the *Al HaNissim* paragraph authorized by the Conservative movement for inclusion in its prayer service for *Yom HaAtzmaut:*

> In the days of destruction of the World War, when Your enemies rose up against Your people to exterminate them as a nation. Six million of our brothers, young and old, were killed. . . . The remnants then rose from the death camps to seek refuge with their brothers who were in the land of their fathers. The gates of their homeland were

closed before them and the seven nations covenanted to destroy Your nation Israel. But You mercifully stood by them in the hour of need.[123]

In reading this paragraph, we see the State as having its roots in the Holocaust, as its growing out of the tragedy of destruction.

But historical coincidence does not make for logical or metaphysical connection. Jews dreamed of a Zionist homeland before Germany unleashed its terror on the world in general and the Jews in particular. *Halutzim* originally came to build the *yishuv* as visionaries, not refugees. The Holocaust may have facilitated the establishment of the State, but the latter, with God's help, was beginning to take form before the destruction.

There were, to be sure, those who saw a logical connection between these two apparently antipodal events. The Satmar community, for example, saw the *Shoah* as a punishment for embracing the Zionist dream.[124] On the other hand, the antithetical position, articulated by Rabbi Yisachar Teichtal[125] (himself a member of this same religious grouping of Hungarian Jewry), saw the *Shoah* as a punishment for rejecting the centrality of Zion in Jewish life. Un-

123. Jules Harlow, ed., *Likutei Tefilah* (New York: The Rabbinical Assembly. 1965), p. 204.

124. See, for example, R. Norman Lamm, "The Ideology of the Neturei Karta According to the Satmar Version," *Tradition*, 12:2 Fall 1971), p. 481.

125. R. Yisachar Shelomo Teichtal, *Eim HaBanim Semaicha*, (Jerusalem: *Makhon Pri HaAretz,* 1983).

able to bring themselves to leave the *galut* and return to their homeland, he argued, the Jews were forced to experience in its cruelest form the reality of their exile. However, these pat explanations somehow don't strike a responsive chord.

The tension of associating *Yom HaShoah* with *Yom HaAtzmaut* can be seen as mirroring the requirement that the *Sheheheyanu* (or *Hatov ve-Hameitiv*) *berakhah* be recited when one hears good news or feels great personal joy (in contrast to the *Dayan Emet* blessing, which is recited when one hears bad news).[126] Theologians might not have worked out the interrelationship of these two events. But the average Jew confronts the horror of the Holocaust with the internal awareness that Israel rose from its ashes, just as he or she tempers the celebration of the birth of the State with the tragic awareness of what Jewry suffered during the period that immediately preceded it. This halakhic model proclaims that this realization must be openly acknowledged even if it is not fully understood.

This is not the only model available to us. In his gloss to this very Halakhah of saying *Sheheheyanu*, Rabbi Akiva Eiger[127] rules that the blessing is not recited by a father who inherits from his deceased son who died childless without other heirs. The magnitude of the tragedy of a father burying a child simply does not allow for acknowledging any positive aspect, however real it might be. So, we might

---

126. *Shulhan Arukh, Orah Hayyim* 222:1–2.
127. Gloss to *Shulhan Arukh, Orah Hayyim* 223:2, s.v. *Mevareikh.*

argue, we are enjoined from infusing *Yom HaShoah* observances with any association with *Yom HaAtzmaut.*

Compare, then, the above *Al HaNissim* with the one
composed for the *Kibbutz HaDati*, the religious kibbutz
movement, one of the major ideological centers of religious
Zionism:

> You aroused the hearts of our fathers to return to the land
> You had granted them, to settle and rebuild it. And when
> the evil regime [England] ruled over us and closed the gates
> of our land to those fleeing a cruel enemy . . . You freed the
> land.[128]

From the perspective of those who came to build the
land in fulfillment of their Torah dreams, the story of the
European destruction insofar as it related to the establishment of the State is just part of the historical situation
which the *yishuv* faced in the late 1940s.

Of course, one might well argue that it is sociology rather
than theology and its various halakhic models that motivated these two distinct liturgical responses. The Conservative movement spoke from a *galut* perspective; indeed, one
might argue that the whole Conservative experience has
been one of reacting to the Western milieu within which it
grew. Supportive of Zionism from afar but participating
directly in the *galut* experience in its everyday life, it saw
the trauma of European Jews as the catalyst for what hap-

---

128. Kibbutz Hadati, *Seder Tefilot LeYom HaAtzmaut* (Tel Aviv:
HaKibbutz HaDati, 1969), p. 101.

pened in the national homeland. The Religious Kibbutz movement, on the other hand, spoke from a Zion-centered perspective. They saw the locus of Jewish history as then centered in the Land of Israel. The destruction in Europe might have been overwhelming in its personal and communal tragic cost. But it was an event played out apart from the drama of the creation of the State.

Of course, sociology is not theology, and we should not rely on it to formulate our philosophic positions. Decades after the State was established in 1948, religious Zionists are still grappling with an understanding of the nature of the *shoah-yeshuah* contrast. The calendar's tension, therefore, should be viewed as a challenge rather than a position, a reflection of a question which will not go away and which ultimately must be addressed

Epilogue:
A Midrash on Jewish Mourning

The Halakhah's approach to dealing with death and tragedy is ensconced in a most famous *aggadita* found in the tractate *Yoma* (69b). The immediate subject of discussion is the *Anshei Knesset Hagedolah*, the "Men of the Great Assembly" who, under the leadership of Ezra the Scribe, reconstituted Judaism after the Return from the Exile following the destruction of the First Temple. They "returned the crown to its lost glory" in their communal response.

Moses had described God as "great, mighty and awesome" (Deut.10:17), and, as we know, this phrase was eventually incorporated into our daily prayers. Yet these qualities were unseen in the hours of destruction and exile. Wishing to confront this cruel reality, the Rabbis seized on two verses with slightly modified descriptions of God. Jeremiah had referred to Him as "great and mighty" in his prayer (Jeremiah 32:18), omitting the phrase "awesome." Daniel had referred to Him as "great and awesome" in his prayer (Daniel 9:4), omitting the term "mighty." The Talmud formulated these verses as a cry and challenge:

Jeremiah said: Gentiles are trampling in His Temple; where
is His awesomeness? He would no longer say "awesome."
Daniel said: Gentiles have enslaved His children; where is
His might? He would no longer say "mighty."

Of course, in marshaling Jeremiah and Daniel to cry out
on the discrepancy between God's attributes and the world
as we know it, the Talmud accomplishes two goals. First,
since it is Jeremiah and Daniel who raise the question, the
"heretical" arguments cannot be dismissed *ad hominem.*
Moreover, by choosing Jeremiah, it makes the point that we
are dealing with an existential crisis and not an intellectual
problem. Jeremiah, after all, knew that the *hurban* was coming; he was intellectually prepared for it. Yet he was shaken
when forced to confront that which he had probably come
to terms with on an intellectual level.

When the *Anshei Knesset HaGedolah* convened to formulate the *Amidah* prayer, they rejected this challenge to the
traditional formulation:

They came and said: On the contrary! It is the culmination
of His might that He represses His inclination to act and
is long-suffering toward the wicked. And if He were not
awesome, how could one nation [the Jews] endure among
the nations of the world?

Of course, it should be noted that no answer was actually
given to the challenges proposed. Jeremiah had asked why
the nations of the world did not recognize God's awesomeness; the response that the Jews did was not relevant to his

question. But the Sages understood that Jeremiah and Daniel were not asking intellectual questions; they were rather expressing a personal crisis. Neither had actively attacked the traditional formulation of God's attributes; indeed, their "challenges" were in the context of a prayer. They simply could not bring themselves to say specific words in light of what they had experienced.

Where could they find the strength? If the Jews could recognize God's awesomeness in the dark period of exile, then, in the context of a believing community, they could draw on the faith of others to get them through the crisis. The community, in a sense, responds and comforts them.

The *aggadita* ends on an interesting note. How, it asks, even in the light of the undeniable facts of human existence, could Jeremiah and Daniel challenge a formulation of God's attributes that dates back to Moses himself?

> R. Eleazar said: They knew that God was truthful; therefore, they would not ascribe false things to Him.

Here we have a succinct summary of a halakhic confrontation with death and suffering: God is a truthful God; He does not want false piety and clichés. Problems have to be confronted, but the solution will not necessarily be found in the realm of the intellect. At times, it is only the vitality of the community that can provide the strength to overcome such existential crises. It is only through the community that the individual mourner can be comforted among all the mourners of Zion and Jerusalem.

אזכרה

אָנָּא יי', הָרוֹפֵא לִשְׁבוּרֵי לֵב וּמְחַבֵּשׁ לְעַצְּבוֹתָם, שַׁלֵּם נִחוּמִים לָאֲבֵלִים.

חַזְּקֵם וְאַמְּצֵם בְּיוֹם אֶבְלָם וִיגוֹנָם, וְזָכְרֵם לְחַיִּים טוֹבִים וַאֲרֻכִּים. תֵּן בְּלִבָּם יִרְאָתְךָ וְאַהֲבָתְךָ לְעָבְדְּךָ בְּלֵבָב שָׁלֵם, וּתְהִי אַחֲרִיתָם שָׁלוֹם, אָמֵן.

כְּאִישׁ אֲשֶׁר אִמּוֹ תְּנַחֲמֶנּוּ
כֵּן אָנֹכִי אֲנַחֶמְכֶם
וּבִירוּשָׁלַיִם תְּנֻחָמוּ:

לֹא-יָבוֹא עוֹד שִׁמְשֵׁךְ, וִירֵחֵךְ לֹא יֵאָסֵף
כִּי יי' יִהְיֶה-לָּךְ לְאוֹר עוֹלָם
וְשָׁלְמוּ יְמֵי אֶבְלֵךְ:

בִּלַּע הַמָּוֶת לָנֶצַח
וּמָחָה אֲדֹנָי יי' דִּמְעָה מֵעַל כָּל-פָּנִים
וְחֶרְפַּת עַמּוֹ יָסִיר מֵעַל כָּל-הָאָרֶץ
כִּי יי' דִּבֵּר:

Memorial Prayer

May the Lord who heals the broken-hearted and binds up their wounds, grant consolation to the mourners.

Strengthen and support them in the day of their sadness and grief, and remember them (and their children) for a long and good life. Put into their hearts love and reverence for You, so that they may serve You with a perfect heart; and let their end be peace. Amen.

As a mother comforts her son,
   so I will comfort you;
   and in Jerusalem you shall find comfort.

Your sun shall no more set,
   your moon shall no more withdraw itself,
   for the Lord shall be your everlasting light,
   and your days of mourning shall be ended.

He will destroy death for ever;
   and the Lord God will wipe away the tears from all faces;
   and remove the reproach of His people from the whole earth;
   for the Lord has spoken it.

Adapted with permission from The Koren Siddur ©2009 Koren Publishers Jerusalem Ltd., English translation ©2009 Rabbi Jonathan Sacks.

Glossary

Aninut: The period of mourning from the relative's death until burial of the deceased

Avel: Mourner (pl. *avelim*)

Avelut: The period of mourning from the time of burial until after *shiva* (or in some cases *sheloshim* or the end of the first twelve months of mourning)

Beraita: The early part of the Talmud not included in the *Mishnah*

Berakhah: Blessing (pl. *berakhot*)

Birkat Avelim: The series of *berakhot* originally said as part of the communal consolation of the mourners

Birkat HaMazon: The series of *berakhot* said after a meal, sometimes referred to as Grace After Meals

Birkat Hatanim: The series of *berakhot* said at the time of a wedding and at communal meals throughout seven days of rejoicing for the couple

Devarim she-be-tzina: Those private activities that are prohibited during the various mourning periods

Galut: Exile from Israel

Gemara: The latter part of the Talmud which functions as a commentary on the Mishnah

Halakhah: The general corpus of Jewish Law, or a specific Jewish law (pl. *halakhot*)

Hesed: A kindness or good deed

Kaddish: The traditional prayer said by mourners throughout their period of mourning and yahrzeit

Keriyah: The ritual tearing of one's clothes as a sign of mourning

125

Kibbud: Honor

Kibbud Ha-met: The honor due a deceased person by virtue of the divine quality of all humans

Mishnah: The early part of the Talmud

Mitzvot: Good deeds or required performances

Nefel: A child who dies within thirty days of birth

Onen: The mourner during the period of *aninut* (pl. *onenim*)

Posek: Rabbinic decisor of Jewish Law (pl. *poskim*)

Shabbat: The Sabbath

Sheloshim: The thirty-day period of mourning that usually begins with *shiva*

Shemua Kerova: News of a relative's death received within thirty days of death

Shemua Rehoka: News of a relative's death received after thirty days of death

Shiva: The seven-day period of mourning that begins at burial

Simha: Joy

Talmud: The main corpus of the Oral Tradition

Zimmun: The blessing recited before *Birkat HaMazon* when the requisite number of people eat together as a community

About the Author

Dr. Joel B. Wolowelsky is Dean of the Faculty at the Yeshivah of Flatbush, where he teaches math and Jewish Philosophy. He is a member of the Steering Committee of the Orthodox Forum and serves on a number of Professional Advisory Boards, including the Bar Ilan University Lookstein Center for Jewish Education in the Diaspora, the Boston Initiative for Excellence in Jewish Day Schools, the Pardes Educators Program in Jerusalem, and Atid: the Academy for Torah Initiatives and Directions. He is associate editor of *Tradition*, the journal of Orthodox Jewish thought published by the Rabbinical Council of America, and the series *MeOtzar HoRav: Selected Writings of Rabbi Joseph B. Soloveitchik.*

BOOKS BY THE AUTHOR

The Mind of the Mourner
Women, Jewish Law and Modernity
Women at the Seder: A Passover Haggadah

BOOKS EDITED OR CO-EDITED

*Abraham's Journey**
The Conversion Crisis
*Days of Deliverance**
*Family Redeemed**
*Festival of Freedom**
Jewish Law and the New Reproductive Technologies
Mind, Body and Judaism
*Out of the Whirlwind**
The Royal Table: A Passover Haggadah
War and Peace in the Jewish Tradition
Women and the Study of Torah
Yavneh Studies in Parashat HaShavua

---

* *MeOtzar HoRav* series